COLLINS GEM

FIRST AID

Dr R. M. Youngson
with
The Diagram Group

HarperCollins*Publishers*

HarperCollins Publishers
PO Box, Glasgow G4 0NB

A Diagram Book first created by Diagram Visual Information Limited of 195 Kentish Town Road, London NW5 8SY

First published 1993

Reprint 10 9 8 7 6

ISBN 0 00 470120 8

All information given in this book has been fully checked and approved by experienced medical and paramedical staff. However, the Collins *Gem First Aid* is not intended as a substitute for professional medical care. It should only be used as a guide to actions that may be needed prior to obtaining appropriate professional treatment.

Printed and bound in Great Britain by
Caledonian International Book Manufacturing Ltd, Glasgow, G64

Introduction

There are many cases where a knowledge of first aid can be useful, and some where it is essential. From minor injuries to major emergencies, a working familiarity with first aid practice can limit injuries sustained by a victim and, in some cases, can actually save a life.

The *Collins Gem First Aid* is clear, informative and user-friendly. It covers a wide variety of injuries and conditions, and enables even the most inexperienced person to provide victims with immediate preliminary aid.

Emergency situations require immediate action and the inexperienced first aider can easily find him- or herself at a loss to know what to do. This book has been designed to help the first aider cope with such situations. Major injuries are clearly distinguished from minor ones; guides to action are distinguished from explanatory information; and 'dos' and 'don'ts' are clearly marked, so that even the lay person can, at a glance, know what to look for and ensure that the best possible preliminary treatment is given to the victim. From removing splinters to coping with heart attacks, from treating headaches to dealing with victims with suspected spinal fractures, the *Collins Gem First Aid* will be an invaluable companion in the home, office or when travelling.

Contents

3. MAJOR INJURIES AND DANGEROUS CONDITIONS

4. MINOR INJURIES AND CONDITIONS

5. DRESSINGS, BANDAGES AND SLINGS

6. USEFUL AIDS

How to use this book

For clear, safe and speedy reference, the various text components of the *Collins Gem First Aid* have been differentiated by the use of colour, and important points have been highlighted using symbols.

The margins of the pages have been colour-coded by chapter, designating relative importance. For example, the pages of Chapter 1, 'The signs of life and emergency techniques', have red margins, while those of Chapter 4, 'Minor injuries and conditions', are pink.

The red text gives step-by-step instructions of what to do when a particular injury or condition is encountered. So that these procedures may be found quickly and easily, an alphabetical list of them has been included on pp.11–16.

The black text offers basic explanatory information about the injuries and conditions, including causes, diagnostic features, and on how certain parts of the body function.

Three symbols are used throughout *First Aid* to draw attention to important points:

✖ caution: action may harm the victim, the first aider or aggravate the injury;

◆ alternative or further procedures and/or tools to be used, if the preceding method has failed, if there are complications or if a particular tool is unavailable;

▶▶ read on: more important text follows.

Procedures of first aid

1. The signs of life and emergency techniques

The signs of life

The signs of life are breathing and the pulse. In emergency situations, the following concerns take priority: **1** that the victim's airway is clear and that they are able to breathe; and **2** that the blood is circulating properly.

A CLEAR AIRWAY

The importance of air supply

The most urgent and immediate responsibility for any person giving first aid is to ensure that the injured person can either breathe freely or is provided artificially with an adequate supply of air. Nothing else is as important as this. Above all, the brain needs oxygen. At normal temperatures, serious brain damage or even death will occur in a matter of minutes if a person ceases to have an adequate intake of air. This may happen because the person has stopped breathing or because the passage along which the air enters the lungs (the airway) has become obstructed.

The first requirement is to check for breathing.

Checking for breathing

Use more than one sense: **1** look for movements of the chest or abdomen – confirm that these are smooth and regular; **2** listen close to the mouth or nose for sounds of breathing; **3** you should be able to feel the victim's breath on your face.

If the casualty is breathing freely you can safely turn your attention to checking for injuries. If the casualty is unconscious and the injuries permit, use the recovery position (see pp. 31–3) to ensure that safe breathing continues.

If there is no breathing

This means that respiration has ceased and you must supply the air. If the chest and abdomen are moving, but there is no movement of air in and out of the mouth or nose, the airway is obstructed and you must clear it. Action is urgently needed to restore the air supply.

Opening the airway

1 The airway may be blocked by the position of the head (**a**). **2** To remedy this, press down on the forehead with one hand, and with the other lift the neck (**b**). **3** Remove your hand from underneath the neck

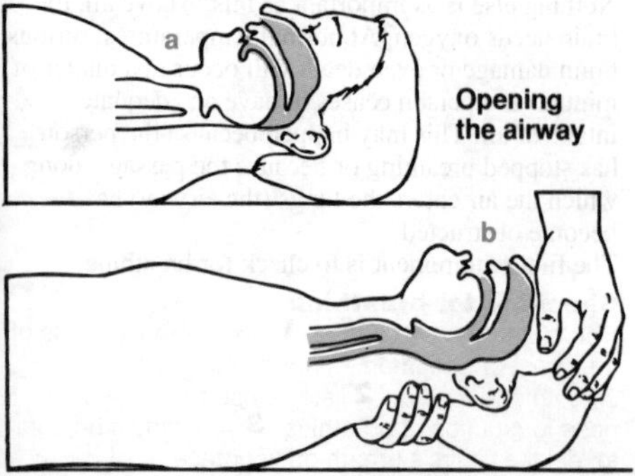

to push the chin up (**c**). This action stops the tongue blocking the top of the airway.

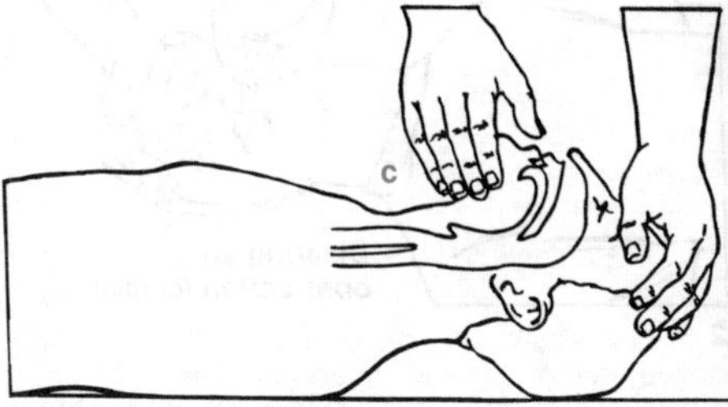

◆ **If there is still no breathing**, there may be an obstruction in the airway.

Clearing an obstruction from the airway

1 Turn the head to one side, keeping the chin forward and the top of the head back (**a**). ►►

Clearing an obstruction

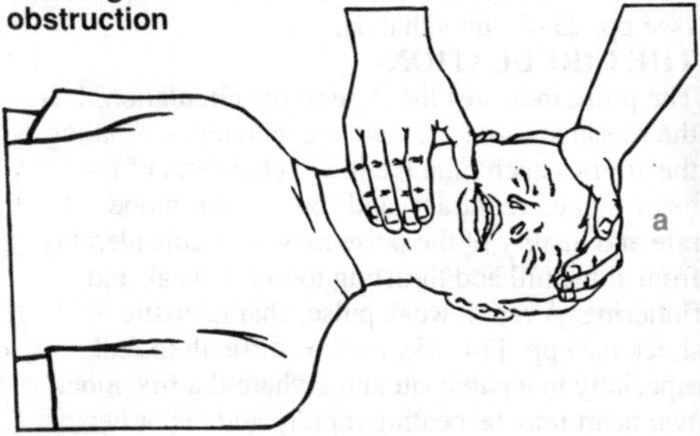

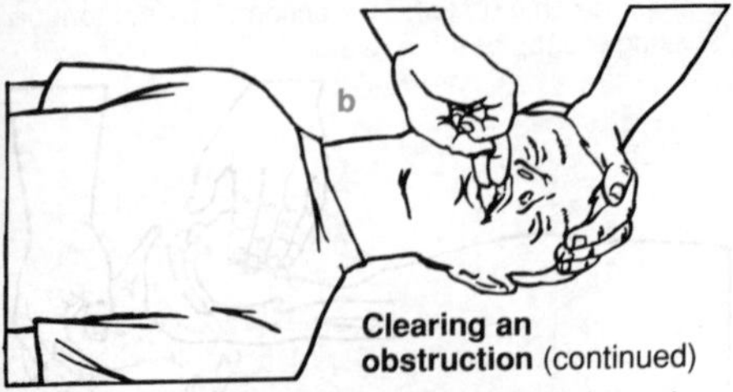

Clearing an obstruction (continued)

2 Sweep around the inside of the mouth above the tongue with two hooked fingers and remove any foreign material (**b**). Do this quickly. Do not waste time. **3** Check for breathing (see pp. 17–18).
4 Check the pulse (opposite).

◆ **If there is still no breathing**, start artificial ventilation at once (see pp. 23–4).

◆ **If there is no breathing *and* no pulse**, start artificial ventilation and external chest compression (see pp. 25–8) immediately.

THE CIRCULATION

The pulse indicates the state of the circulation. It is the repeated, brief pressure wave that passes along the arteries each time the lower chambers of the heart tighten (contract) and squeeze out blood. The rate and quality of the pulse may vary considerably, from slow, full and thrusting to rapid, weak and fluttering. A rapid, weak pulse, characteristic of shock (see pp. 114–15), may be difficult to feel, especially in a panic situation where the first aider's own heart may be beating rapidly and his or her pulse may be much stronger than that of the victim.

For this reason, feeling the pulse at the usual site, on the thumb side of the wrist, 1.5 cm above the wrist crease and 1.5 cm in from the edge (**a**), may not be reliable. So you should always feel for the carotid pulse in the neck. The carotids are large arteries that run up on either side of the back of the Adam's apple (larynx) (**b**).

Checking the pulse

1 Breathe deeply to calm yourself, if necessary. **2** Use only the tips of two fingers. Place them on the side of the Adam's apple without pressing on it. **3** Slide your fingertips firmly backwards along the side of the Adam's apple so that they pass into the vertical groove between it and the muscle to the side of it (**c**). **4** If you do not immediately feel the pulse, move the fingertips a little nearer to and further from the Adam's apple until the pulse is felt.

The pulse

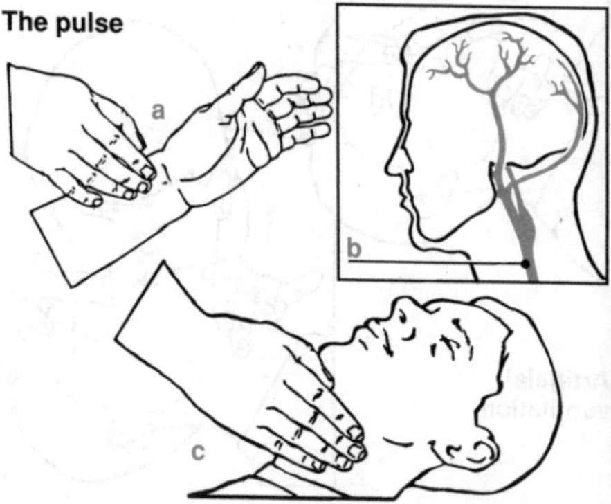

Emergency techniques

ARTIFICIAL VENTILATION

The object of this is to provide the victim immediately with an air supply. The air you breathe out still has adequate amounts of oxygen for someone else to use. Many lives have been saved with 'second-hand' oxygen. There must be no delay in starting artificial ventilation and you must be sure that the air is getting to the right place – deep into the lungs of the victim.

It is essential that you succeed in inflating the lungs. If you do not see the chest rising when you blow and falling when you stop, you are not succeeding; you may have to follow the procedure for choking (see pp. 76–83).

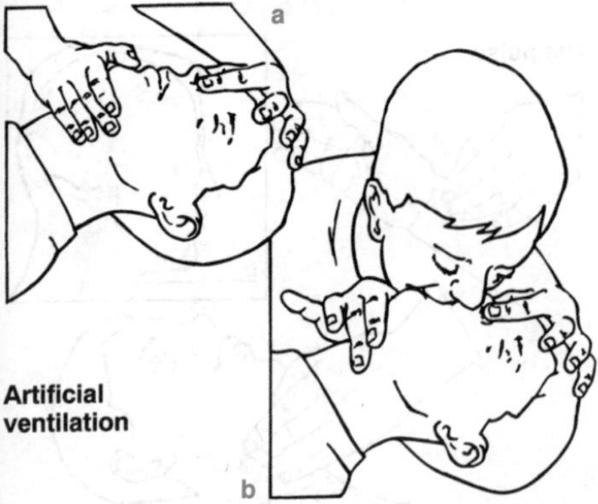

Artificial ventilation

✖ **Care must be taken** when performing this technique. Deaths have occurred where obstructions in the airway have been blown deeper into the lungs.

Giving artificial ventilation

1 Check the pulse (see p. 21). **2** If there is no heartbeat start chest compression (see pp. 25–8). **3** If there is a pulse clear the mouth of foreign material (see pp. 19–20). **4** Push the chin up with one hand and tilt back the head. **5** Pinch the nose closed (**a**). **6** Take a deep breath, open your mouth wide and seal it around the victim's mouth (**b**). **7** Blow strongly into the mouth while watching for the chest to rise (**c**). **8** Once the chest has risen, turn your head to watch the chest fall (**d**); finish breathing out. Give the first four breaths quickly. **9** Check the pulse. **10** Repeat actions 5 to 9 until the victim starts to breathe again. ►►

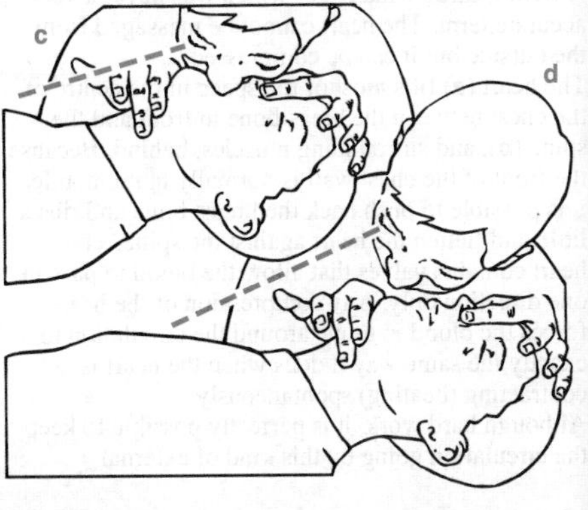

An alternative to mouth-to-mouth resuscitation (if, for some reason, it is impossible) is mouth-to-nose. Close or cover the mouth firmly and blow into the nose, ensuring a good seal.

♦ **If the chest does not rise**, make the following checks.

Checks

1 That the nose is properly closed. **2** That the seal around the mouth or nose is tight. **3** That you are blowing hard enough.

♦ **If, in spite of all, you are not succeeding**, then there must be an airway obstruction (see pp. 19–20 and 76–83 for action).

EXTERNAL CHEST COMPRESSION

This is the procedure to follow if there is no pulse (see p. 21). Chest compression used to be called 'external cardiac massage' which was never a very accurate term. The heart cannot be massaged from the outside but it can be compressed.

The heart (**a**) fills most of the space in the centre of the chest between the breastbone in front and the spine (**b**), and surrounding muscles, behind. Because the front of the chest wall is normally quite mobile, it is possible to push back the breast bone and ribs a little and flatten the heart against the spine. The heart contains valves that allow the blood to pass in one direction only. Any compression of the heart forces the blood to move around the circulation in exactly the same way it does when the heart is contracting (beating) spontaneously.

Although hard work, it is perfectly possible to keep the circulation going by this kind of external

Position of the heart

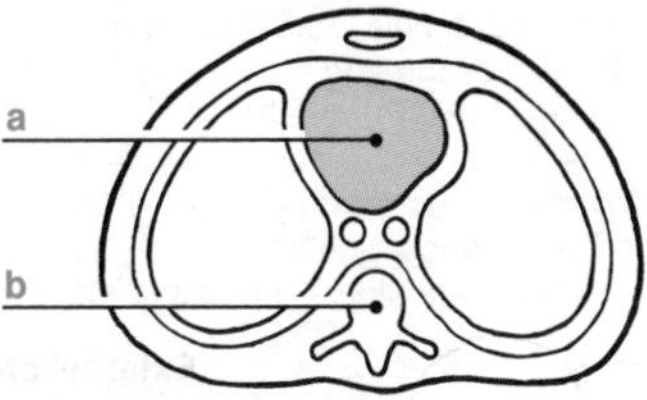

compression. So long as air is, at the same time, being forced into the lungs, there is a good chance that the skin will regain its healthy colour, the dilated pupils of the eyes will constrict, and that other signs of apparent recovery will occur (see p. 28). If the victim is capable of recovering, this procedure will often restart the spontaneous heartbeat and restore spontaneous breathing. External heart compression without mouth-to-mouth ventilation, however, is futile. The purpose of the exercise is to restore the circulation of blood containing oxygen. So you must also supply the oxygen.

✖ **Extreme caution** is required when performing this technique. The heartbeat must have completely stopped before external chest compression is given; otherwise, a faintly beating heart may be stopped by this procedure.

✖ **The following procedure** should only be performed by a trained first aider.

Performing external chest compression

1 Lay the victim flat on his back and kneel alongside. **2** Feel for the angle of the ribs at the bottom of the chest (**a**). Put the heel of one hand on the breastbone, two finger-breadths above the angle. **3** Cover your hand with your other hand. The thumbs and fingers should be kept raised. Lean forward so that your shoulders are above the

External chest compression

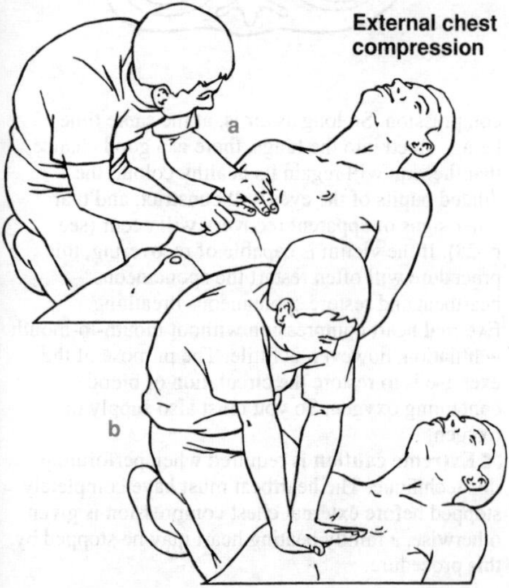

breastbone. Keep your arms straight (**b**). **4** Press vertically down (**c**), depressing the front chest wall by 4–5 cm ($1\frac{1}{2}$–2 in). This is the distance for an adult. Move the wall 2.5–4 cm (1–$1\frac{1}{2}$ in) for a child. Compress the chest in this way 15 times, at a rate that is faster than one push per second. Time the compressions by counting 'one, two, three' steadily, compressing on each 'one'. **5** Move to the victim's head and give him two effective mouth-to-mouth puffs (**d**) to get air into the lungs (see p. 23). ►►

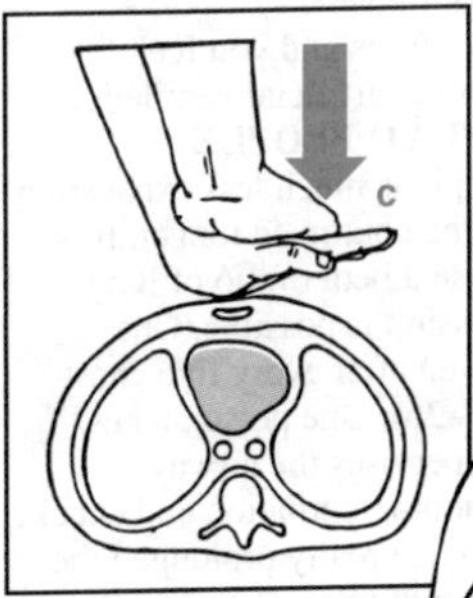

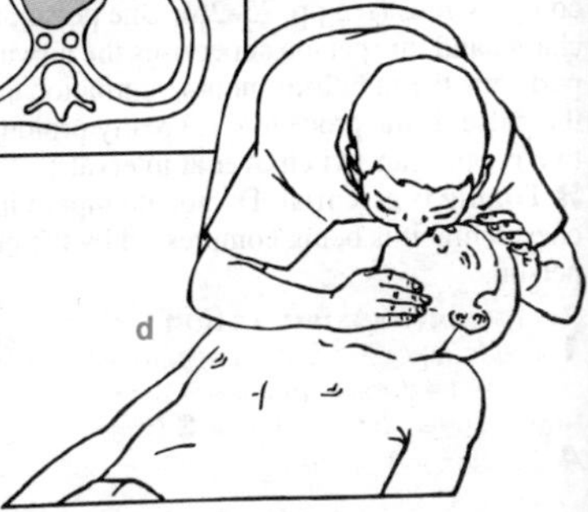

6 Remember to watch the chest movements. **7** Repeat the cycle of 15 compressions and two lung inflations until the victim shows signs of recovery, until help arrives or until you are exhausted. **8** Check the pulse in the neck (see p. 21) every 3 minutes.

Signs of recovery

- The blue, grey or purplish skin colour disappears and the skin regains its healthy colour.
- The pulse returns.
- The victim may groan or move.
- Spontaneous breathing returns and you feel resistance when performing artificial ventilation.

RESUSCITATION BY TWO PEOPLE

Resuscitation by two people is much less exhausting than it is for one and can be continued longer. It is also more efficient because a better ratio of lung inflation to chest compression is possible. One inflation (see p. 23) is given after every five chest compressions (see pp. 25–26). One person takes charge and this person supervises the airway, performs the mouth-to-mouth ventilation and checks the pulse. If the procedure is greatly prolonged the two people can switch over at intervals.

✖ **Timing is essential**. Do not attempt to inflate the chest while it is being compressed by the other person.

Performing resuscitation

1 The first person should ensure that the airway is clear, and establish that there is no breathing. **2** Start with two inflations (**a**). **3** Check the pulse. **4** The second person gives five chest compressions (**b**). **5** Give one inflation every time the fifth compression is released. **6** Repeat steps 4 and 5 until the victim starts to recover or until professional help arrives. **7** Check the neck pulse every two minutes (**c**).

Resuscitation by two people

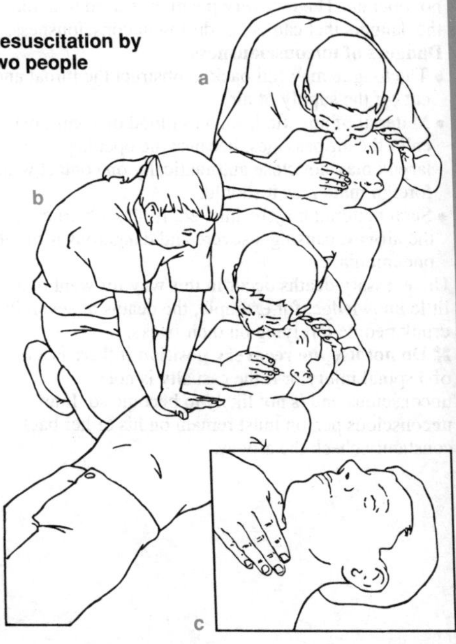

THE RECOVERY POSITION

When unconscious or semi-conscious people are left lying on their backs, they are in serious danger. This is because the muscles are relaxed and the normal reflexes that ensure an open and clear airway may not operate. The recovery position is used to avoid the dangers that can occur during unconsciousness.

Dangers of unconsciousness

- The tongue may fall back to obstruct the throat and cut off the supply of air.
- Material of any kind, such as blood or vomit, may enter the air passages, because the opening to the larynx may not close automatically on contact with foreign matter, as it should.
- Such material may be inhaled, further obstructing the airway, causing a severe and dangerous form of pneumonia.

Unnecessary deaths occur in this way for want of a little knowledge, for example, the deaths of severely drunk people left lying on their backs.

✘ **Do not use the recovery position** if there is a risk of a spinal injury or if the casualty is not unconscious and is not likely to become so. If an unconscious person must remain on his or her back, constantly check the airway.

Putting a person in the recovery position
1 Kneel to one side of the victim. **2** Straighten the arm nearest to you and tuck it under the victim's body (**a**). **3** Bring the arm farthest from you across the chest, holding the palm of this arm against the victim's cheek nearest you (**b**). ►►

The recovery position

a

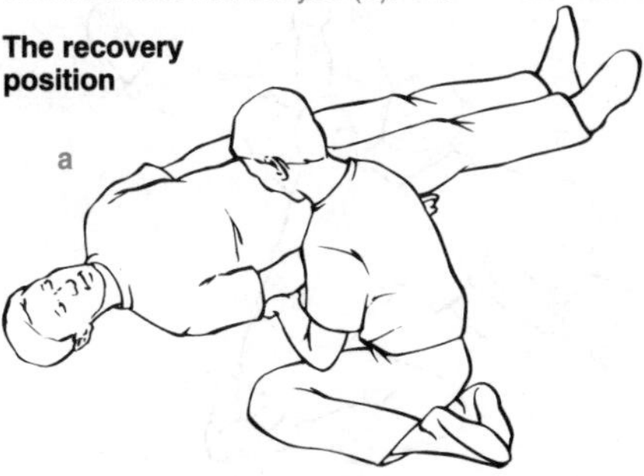

b

4 Holding the palm against the victim's cheek, raise the knee furthest from you (**c**). **5** Gently pull on the knee, turning the casualty toward you (**d**).

The recovery position (continued)

c

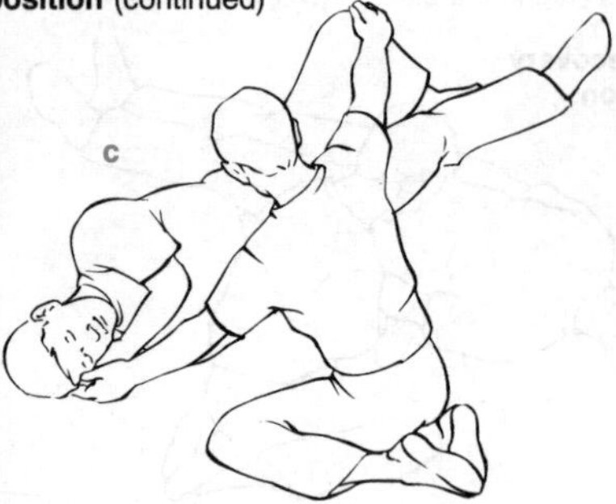

d

6 On the side to which the victim's head is turned, make sure the knee remains at right angles to the body (**e**). **7** Push the head back to ensure a clear airway and check the breathing (**f**).

✖ Do not leave the victim unattended.

e

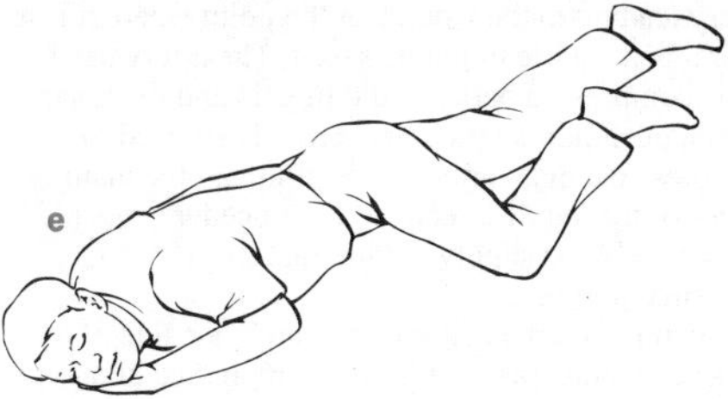

f

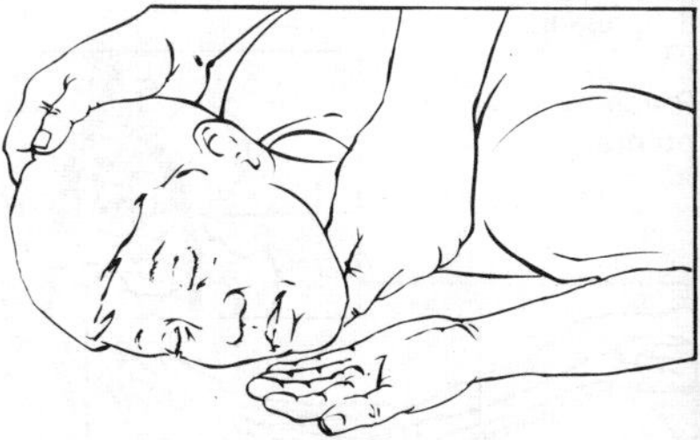

SEVERE BLEEDING AND PRESSURE POINTS

In desperate cases, where severe bleeding continues, in spite of direct pressure a pad or a bandage (see pp. 70–1) being applied to the wound, the flow of arterial blood may have to be stopped for a while but only as a last resort. By using indirect pressure on the artery leading to the wound, at the point where it runs over a bone, a life might be saved. The artery needs to be compressed between the fingers and the bone. In practice, indirect pressure can only be used to compress the main artery of the arm and the main artery of the leg. If effective, the procedure cuts off the whole blood supply to the limb.

Pressure points

The main arm artery runs down the inner side of the upper arm bone (**a**), and is best compressed about the middle of the bone.

The main leg artery enters the leg at about the middle of the fold of the groin. At this point, it runs over a bony ridge on the pelvis (**b**), where it is best to apply the pressure.

Pressure points

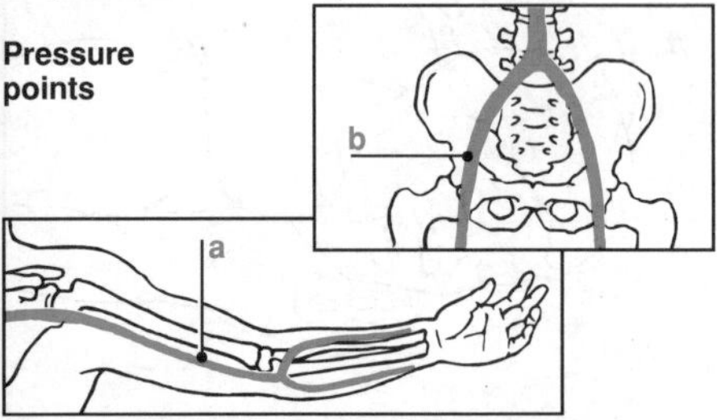

✖ **Do not cut off arterial blood supply** for more than 15 minutes at a time, otherwise there is danger of death (gangrene) of healthy tissue beyond the point of pressure.

✖ **Never use tourniquets.**

Stopping arm bleeding

1 Hold the injured arm so the hand is raised above the victim's head. **2** Press your fingertips firmly inwards and upwards between the muscles, on the inside of the upper arm, until you can feel the bone (**a**) and see that the bleeding is greatly reduced.

Stopping leg bleeding

1 The victim should be lying down with the knees slightly bent. **2** You must press the artery firmly against the pelvic bone with the heel of your hand or, if you are sure of the location, with your thumbs (**b**). Strong pressure is necessary to compress this large artery.

Stopping bleeding

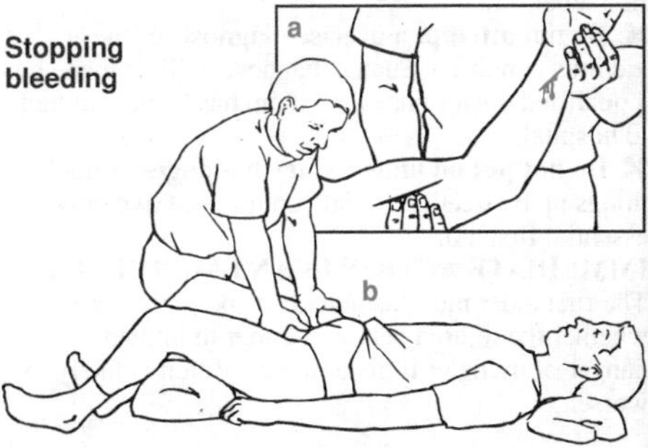

2. Emergency management of serious injuries

Principles and responsibilities

THE JOB OF THE FIRST AIDER

The priorities, in order, are:

- always to avoid endangering yourself;
- to ensure that the victim is safe from danger, by moving him or her if necessary (see pp. 43–60);
- to check the victim's condition and assess his or her injuries;
- to take immediate remedial action if necessary.

✖ **Do not try to do too much**: remember that ambulance paramedics will know more than the lay first aider.

✖ **Do not attempt a precise diagnosis** of the victim's condition. Such a diagnosis will be made by a qualified doctor once the victim has been admitted to hospital.

✖ **Do not put on unnecessary bandages** or hold things up by treating trivial conditions. Give only essential first aid.

IMMEDIATE ACTION IN AN EMERGENCY

The first aider must, as quickly as possible, assess whether the injured person is either in immediate danger of dying or if his or her condition is likely to worsen.

Checking the victim's condition
Check **1** that there is no obstruction of the airway (**a**) (see pp. 19–20); **2** that the victim is breathing (**b**) (see pp. 17–18); **3** that there is a pulse (**c**) (to make sure cardiac arrest has not occurred); **4** for severe bleeding; **5** for shock (see p. 113).

Checking the victim's condition

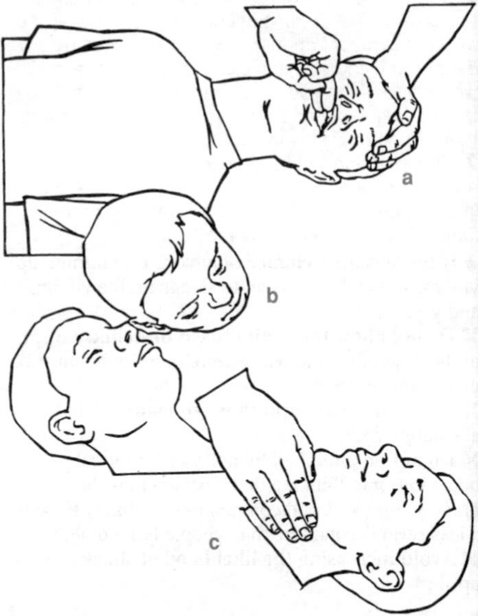

Taking remedial action

1 A blocked airway: see 'Opening the airway', pp. 18–19. **2** Air supply: see 'Checking for breathing', pp. 17–18, and 'Artificial ventilation', pp. 23–4. **3** Cardiac arrest: see 'External chest compression', pp. 25–8. **4** Severe bleeding: see 'Severe bleeding and pressure points', pp. 34–5. **5** Shock: see pp. 114–15. **6** Ask someone else (if possible) to call an ambulance (see p. 40) as soon as you have confirmed that the victim is not in danger of dying or that his or her condition is worsening. If the you are alone with the victim and there is a good chance of someone else turning up, then you should stay to maintain the checks.

7 Reassure the victim. Remain calm at all times, and do whatever possible to reassure a conscious injured person that he or she will soon be properly looked after and on the way to recovery.

♦ **If there is little chance** of anyone else turning up, you must do what you can to safeguard the victim, and go for help.

✖ **Do not allow the victim to eat or drink**, except in the case of people with severe burns, who must be given sips of water.

✖ **Never move an injured person** unless it is absolutely necessary.

✖ **Do not be panicked** by noisy or hysterical behaviour into thinking that a person must be gravely injured. Loud complainers are likely to be in a less serious condition than people lying quietly.

✖ **Avoid increasing the likelihood of shock** (see pp. 114–15).

SPECIFIC INJURIES AND CONDITIONS

Burns and scalds

Minimize the damage from burns and scalds by removing burning clothing and cooling the burned parts as quickly as possible with water (see pp. 92–3). Hot, wet clothing may continue to burn and should be dowsed with water before removal.

✘ **Do not remove burned clothing** if it has adhered to the victim's skin.

Wound infection

Open wounds must be covered in order to reduce the risk of wound infection (see pp. 178–9).

Unconscious victim

The airway of an unconscious victim must be safeguarded (see pp. 17–20).

Fractures

Further damage from broken bones (fractures) must be prevented by immobilizing the affected limb, so that movement at the fracture site is minimized, and further tissue injury avoided (see pp. 132–58).

✘ **Avoid using improvised splints** if an ambulance is on its way: ambulance paramedics will have better equipment for splinting fractures.

Body temperature

Wrap the victim in a blanket in order to maintain his or her body temperature.

✘ **Do not allow the victim to get too hot** by wrapping him or her up in too many layers or by using a hot-water bottle – this may cause skin flushing, because of widened blood vessels, and precipitate shock.

WHAT THE EMERGENCY SERVICES NEED TO KNOW

First aiders or their assistants, after having dialled 999 and asked for the appropriate service, must pass on the following essential information.

Essential information

- The number from which they are calling, so that they can be contacted again if necessary.
- The exact location or address of the incident. Local road names and the postal district, if known. Proximity to road junctions or to any conspicuous landmarks.
- The nature of the incident, its severity and its seeming degree of urgency.
- The nature of the injuries or illnesses.
- The number, age and sex of people injured.

The HIV risk

It is necessary today to consider the possibility that an injured and bleeding person may be HIV positive and may offer a risk of infection to someone providing first aid. This risk is smaller than commonly supposed, as the following examples show.

Examples

- Very few medical and paramedical people have been infected by victims who are HIV positive. In those cases where infection has occurred, it has been transmitted via cuts or punctures which have become contaminated by the victim's infected blood.
- Surgeons engaged in operations on victims

from areas of high AIDS prevalence, have, in about 8 per cent of cases, had direct skin contact with infected blood. Only a tiny number of these, however, have actually become infected themselves.

It is unlikely that a victim receiving first aid is HIV positive, and even if he or she is, the chances of a first aider actually acquiring the infection from such a person are very small.

Nevertheless, because the consequences of HIV infection are so serious, certain elementary precautions must always be taken.

Precautions

- Spilled blood should be assumed to be infected, and it is strongly advised that contact with it should be avoided, if possible. There is a small but real danger of infection if HIV-positive blood contaminates cuts or abrasions possessed by a first aider.
- If the skin of a first aider comes into contact with a large quantity of the victim's blood, then the blood should be wiped away and the skin washed at the earliest possible opportunity. The risk of being infected in this way is, however, very small.
- First aiders must try to avoid getting blood in their eyes: though the risk is small, HIV infection can occur through the membrane that covers the whites of the eyes (the conjunctiva). Any visible blood should be washed out.
- The risk from saliva contamination during mouth-to-mouth artificial ventilation (see pp. 23–4) is believed to be negligible. It is probably a little

greater, however, if there is bleeding around the victim's mouth. In this situation, it is necessary to give the victim's mouth a quick clean before starting. If the risk still seems real, then the following procedure can be used.

Avoiding HIV infection when there are facial injuries

1 Cut a small slit in a thin polythene bag. **2** Place the bag on the victim's face, so that the slit is over the victim's mouth. This will enable mouth-to-mouth artificial respiration to take place without the first aider's mouth coming into skin-to-skin contact with that of the victim. **3** Perform artificial ventilation (see pp. 23–4) by blowing through the slit.

Avoiding HIV infection

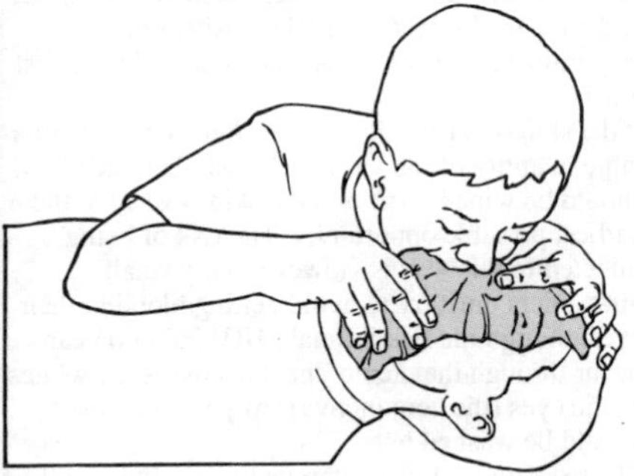

Moving and lifting victims

The primary considerations for the first aider are to safeguard the victim's well being and ensure that he or she is comfortable. The victim's condition must not be aggravated, nor their life endangered, by careless handling.

WHEN TO MOVE AN INJURED PERSON

An injured person should be moved only when medical help is not readily available, or when there is immediate danger to life. The following are examples of situations where it may be necessary to move victims.

Examples

- On a busy road which cannot be blocked off.
- In a dangerous building, perhaps threatened by fire or possibility of collapse.
- In a building containing gas or poisonous fumes, such as a garage full of carbon monoxide (see p. 85).

Before you move an injured person

- If it is necessary to move the victim, then try first to assess the nature and severity of the injuries, if this is at all possible. Examine the head and neck, chest and abdomen, and all limbs which, if injured, must be supported during removal.
- If there is any doubt about the severity of injuries in an injured (but conscious and freely breathing) person who has to be moved, then aim to move the victim in exactly the position in which he or she was found. ►►

✖ **Avoid moving a person** with a severe crush injury – it may do great harm (see pp. 116–17).
✖ **Single first aiders** should never attempt to move victims by themselves when help is available.

GENERAL RULES FOR LIFTING

The following principles should always be adhered to in all cases where victims have to be lifted.

Principles

A first aider must
- get close to the victim;
- keep the feet comfortably apart, to ensure a firm stance and a stable, balanced posture;
- lower him- or herself to the victim's level by bending the knees, not the back;
- keep the back straight;
- grasp the victim firmly, using the whole hand;
- lift with the legs, not the back, and use the shoulders to support the weight of the victim.

Lifting posture

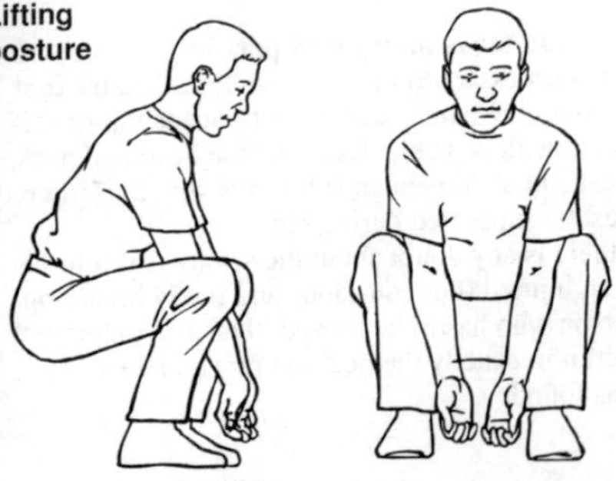

♦ **If the victim begins to slip**, let him or her slide gently to the ground, to avoid causing further injury.
✖ **Do not try to prevent** the casualty falling: this may lead to injury to your back.
✖ **Do not try to lift** too heavy a weight – get assistance whenever possible: the larger the group of people lifting the victim, the smaller the chances of causing or incurring injury.

WHICH METHOD TO USE

Various methods are used to move or lift injured persons. The method to be used in any particular situation depends on the following points:

- the number of available helpers;
- the size and weight of the victim;
- the distance the victim has to be carried;
- the terrain across which the victim has to be moved;
- the type and the severity of the injury sustained by the victim;
- the equipment and amenities available to the first aider.

ONE FIRST AIDER

Dragging the victim

This method should only be used when the victim cannot be lifted, is not capable of standing up, and has to be moved quickly. It is performed in the following way.

Method (see overleaf)
1 Fold the victim's arms across the chest (**a**).
2 Pull back the victim's unbuttoned overcoat or jacket and place it underneath the head (**b**). ►►

3 Crouch down behind the victim, grasp the shoulders of the clothing, and tug the victim smoothly away (**c**).

Dragging the victim

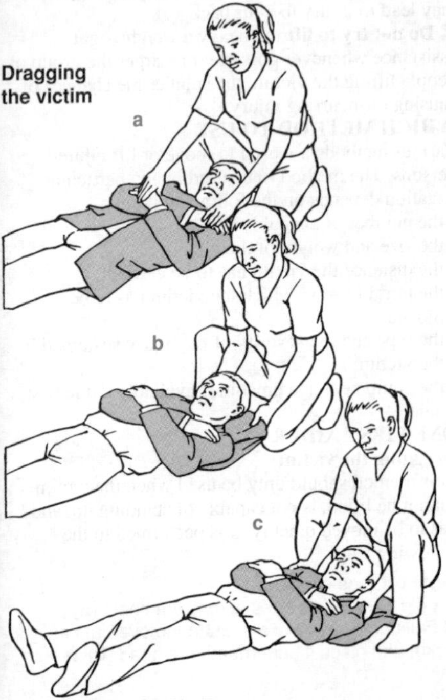

◆ **If the victim is not wearing a jacket** or an overcoat, then you must hold the victim underneath the armpits and tug. Use your arms to cradle the victim's head.

If the victim has no jacket

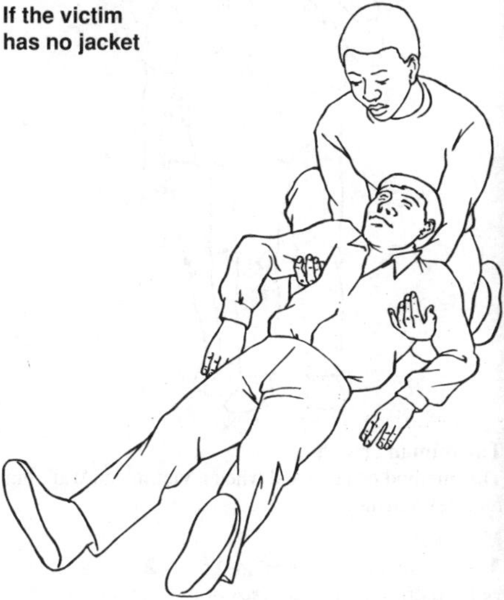

The human crutch

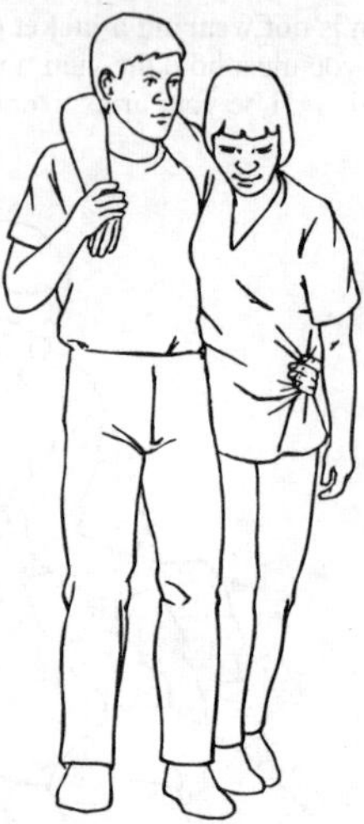

The human crutch
This method can be used when a victim can walk but requires assistance.

Method

1 Stand at the victim's injured side. **2** Place the victim's arm round your neck and hold the victim's hand. **3** Put the other arm round the victim's waist, grasping the clothing at the hip.

✖ **Do not use this method** if the victim has received an injury to the upper limbs.

The cradle **Pickaback**

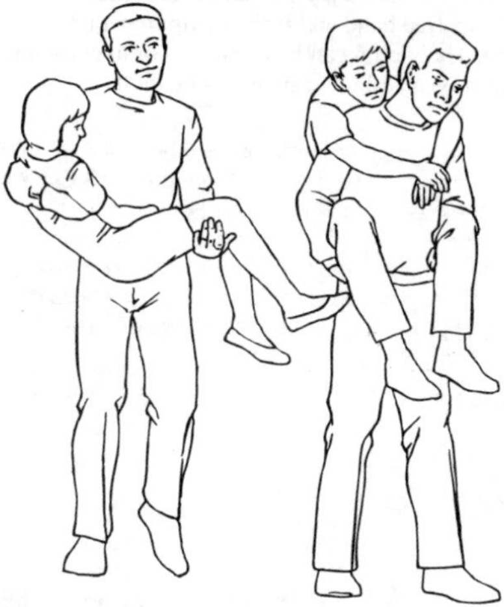

The cradle

This method is suitable for children or victims who are not heavy.

Method

Carry the victim by placing one arm under the thighs, and the other above the waist.

Pickaback

A small, light and conscious victim, who is strong enough to hold on to a first aider, may be carried in pickaback fashion.

The fireman's lift

This method can be used when the first aider requires a free hand and if the victim must be moved. The victim can be conscious or unconscious, but must be a child or a lightweight adult.

Method

1 Help the victim to stand. **2** Take hold of the victim's right wrist with your left hand (**a**). **3** Bend your knees, bend forward, and carefully put your right shoulder into the victim's groin, letting the victim fall gently across your shoulders. **4** Put your right arm around and behind the victim's knees (**b**). **5** Stand up and adjust the victim's weight across your shoulders (**c**).

The fireman's lift

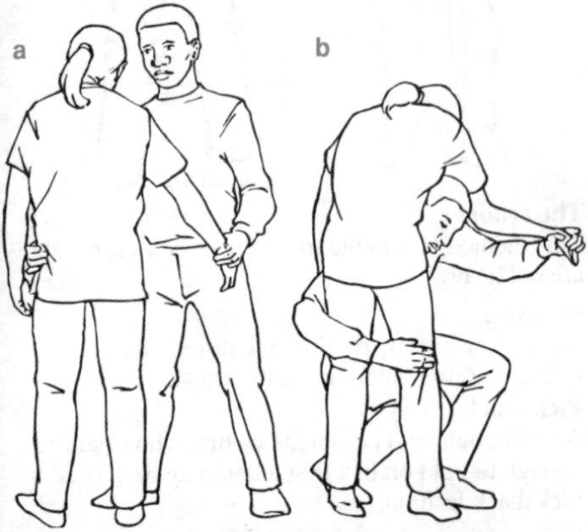

c

◆ **If the victim cannot stand,** he or she must be turned face-down, if necessary, and pulled up on to his or her knees and then into a standing position. Stand close and lift by passing your arms under the victim's armpits.

If the victim cannot stand

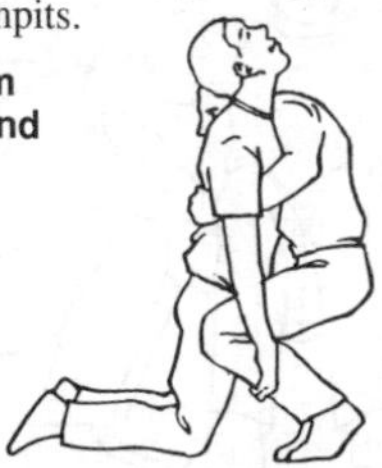

TWO FIRST AIDERS

Two people, lifting together, can provide a carrier seat for a victim.

The four-handed seat

This method is used when the victim is in a condition to use one or both arms to assist the first aiders.

Method

1 Each person grasps his or her own left wrist with the right hand, and then the other's right wrist with the left hand (**a**). **2** Both squat down. **3** The victim sits on their hands and puts an arm round each person's neck (**b**). **4** Both carriers rise together. **5** The carriers step out simultaneously, stepping first with their outside feet, and walk forward at an ordinary pace.

The four-handed seat

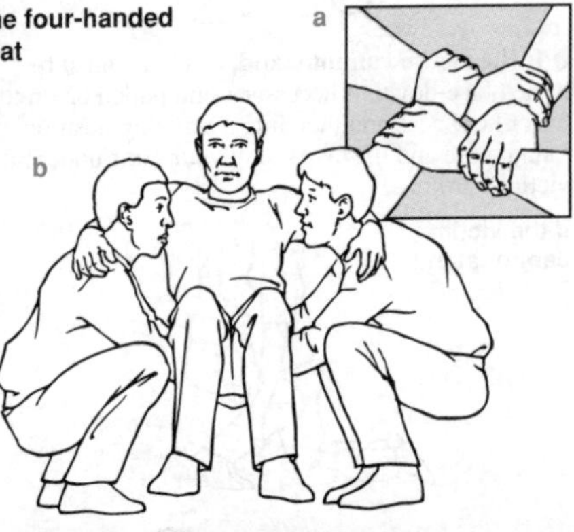

Two-handed seat

This seat is used to transport a victim who is unable to assist the first aiders, usually because of injury to the arms.

Method

1 Two first aiders squat facing each other on either side of the victim. **2** They pass the forearms nearest to the victim's body under the victim's back, just below the shoulders, and grasps the victim's clothing (**a**). **3** The first aiders slightly raise the victim's back, pass their other arms under the middle of the victim's thighs and grasp each other's wrists (**b**). **4** The first aiders rise simultaneously, start walking using the feet on the outside, and continue at an ordinary pace.

The two-handed seat

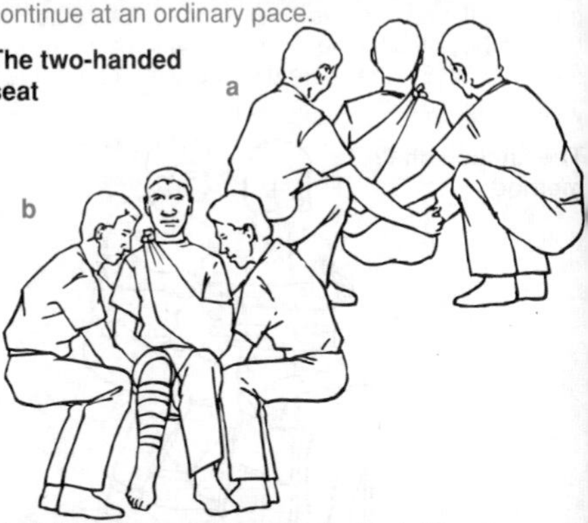

♦ **If there is no clothing** for the first aiders to grasp, then they must, if possible, grasp each other's wrists.

The kitchen chair method

When a victim has to be moved along passageways, or up and down stairs, the kitchen chair method is most suitable. The victim must be conscious and must not have serious injuries.

Method

1 Test the chair to ensure that it can comfortably carry the victim's weight. **2** Ensure that the way is cleared of all obstructions, such as loose carpeting. **3** Secure the trunk and thighs of the victim to the chair with scarves or large bandages (**a**). **4** First aiders should stand at the front and rear of the chair, and tilt it backwards (to an angle of about 30° from the horizontal) before lifting it (**b**). **5** One first aider supports the back of the chair and the victim; the other (who is facing the victim) holds the chair by its front legs and moves carefully backwards down the stairs or along the passageway.

The kitchen chair method

a

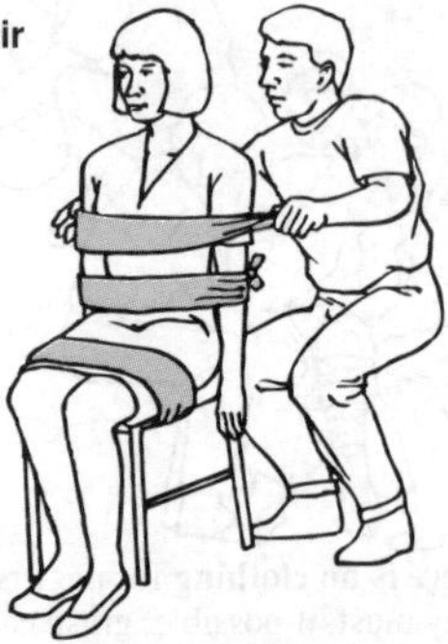

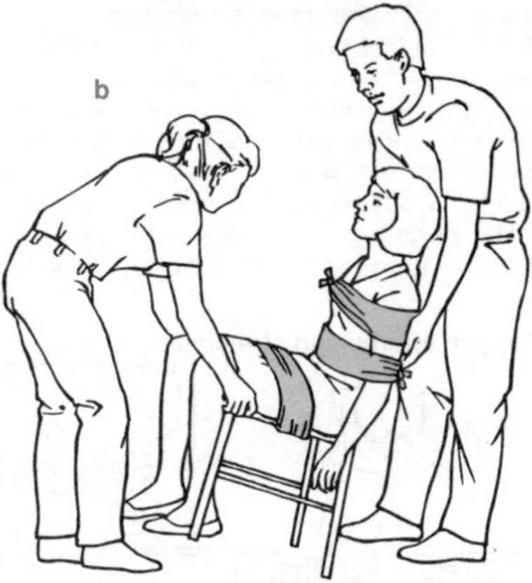

◆ **If the stairs or passageway** are sufficiently wide, the first aiders can stand by the sides of the chair, each holding one back and one front chair leg.

✖ **Never tilt the chair** without previously informing the victim: neglecting to do so risks causing the victim further injury and distress.

Stretchers

Stretchers are useful for moving victims over long distances. The stretcher here described is an improvised model and the method for removal is suitable for two people. As a general rule, try always to ensure, when using a stretcher, that the position of the victim's head and neck is aligned with his or her body, and make sure that the airway is unobstructed.

Making an improvised stretcher

1 Find two or three strong jackets or coats. **2** Turn the sleeves of the coats inside out and pass a strong pole (such as a broomstick) through one of the sleeves of each jacket (**a**), and a second pole through the others. **3** Button or zip up the jackets to complete the stretcher (**b**). **4** Test the stretcher, if possible, by getting an uninjured person to lie on it, and then lift it to ensure that it can safely handle the weight.

Making an improvised stretcher

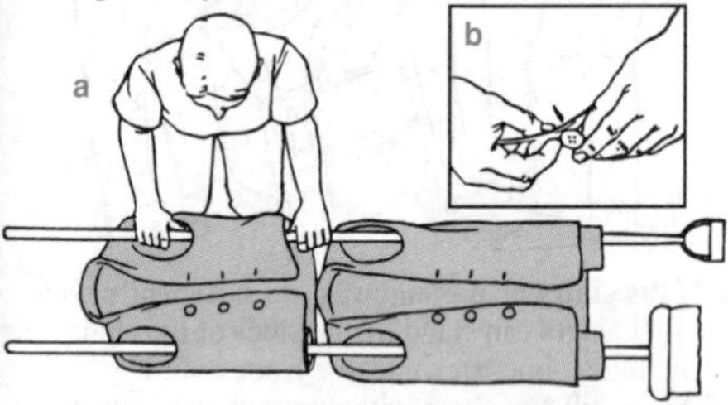

◆ **If a blanket is available**, it should be draped across the stretcher before the victim is placed on it, Wrap it around the victim when he or she has been placed on the stretcher.

◆ **If strong jackets or coats are not available**, then try the substitutes listed below.

- Strong sacks: make holes in the bottom corners of one or more sacks. Pass the poles through them.
- Broad bandages: these can be firmly tied, at intervals, to two poles.

- A strong blanket, tarpaulin, rug or piece of sacking: spread the material out, lay the poles in place and fold the material over from both sides so that the weight of the victim keeps it in place.

Moving a victim on to a stretcher

1 One first aider must carefully roll the victim on to the uninjured side. **2** The other first aider must then place the open stretcher flat against the victim's back. **3** Carefully roll the stretcher, with the victim now lying on it, back onto the floor before lifting it up.

◆ **If the victim is unconscious**, position the open stretcher against the victim's front, and carry him or her in the recovery position (see pp. 31–3).

Moving a victim on to a stretcher

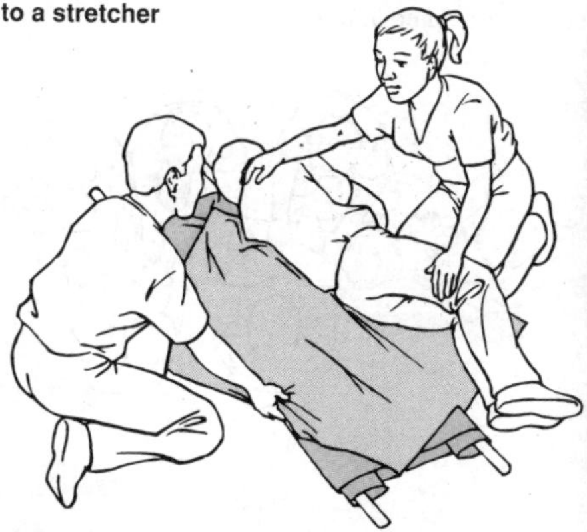

MORE THAN TWO FIRST AIDERS

Turning a victim with suspected spine injury

It is necessary to turn such a victim on to his or her side when he or she is vomiting, to ensure that the victim does not choke on his or her own vomit, and to avoid any distress or discomfort which could cause them to move, and possibly further exacerbate the injury.

Six people are required to perform this task.

Method

Three people must hold the victim on one side, two on the other and one at the head. Turn the victim very carefully, without any twisting or bending of the spine.

Turning a victim with suspected spine injury

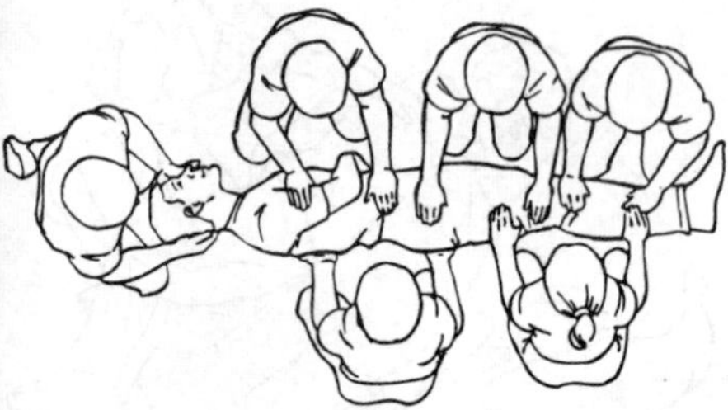

✖ **Never ever allow the victim's head** to move out of alignment with their body.

Moving a victim with suspected spine fracture

Seven people are required to make such a removal.

Method

1 Firmly hold the victim's head, shoulders and pelvis and place pads of soft material between the ankles, knees and thighs (**a**). **2** Tie the victim's legs together. The feet should be tied together with a figure-of-eight bandage (see p. 239) (**b**; see overleaf). **3** Position three people on each side of the victim. **4** The remaining first aider must then squat at the head of the victim (looking down the axis of the victim's body), and keep the victim's head and neck aligned; this is achieved by carefully placing a hand on either side of the victim's head. The person at the head gives the orders to the lifters. ►►

Moving a victim with suspected spine fracture

a

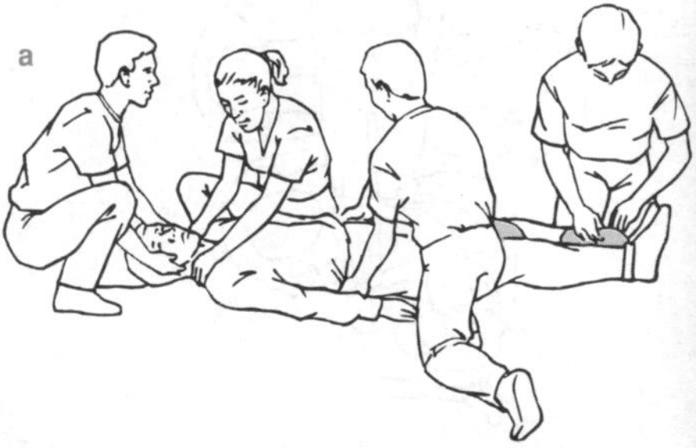

5 Roll the victim slightly, so that the lifters can get their arms under the victim's body (**c**). ►►

Moving a victim with suspected spine fracture (continued)

b

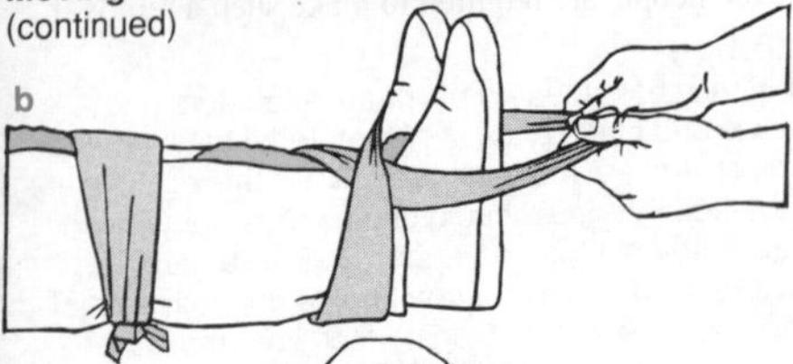

c

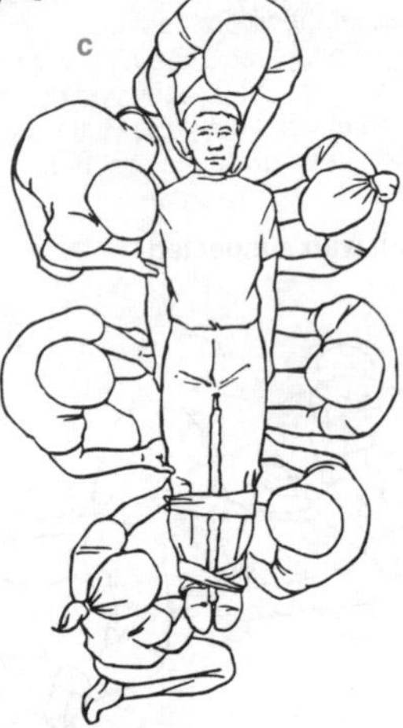

✖ **Never ever allow the victim's head** to move out of alignment with the body.

Removing clothing and helmets

REMOVING CLOTHING

It is sometimes necessary to remove clothing in order to perform proper treatment, reveal injuries or to obtain a clear diagnosis of the victim's condition. Many injuries, however, can be inspected without having to resort to clothes removal: fractures can readily be diagnosed without removing clothing, and major wounds are unlikely to have occurred without obvious tearing of the clothing.

If clothing must be removed, then take off only the minimum amount and try to disturb the victim as little as possible. Always ask a conscious victim's permission before removing clothing.

Removal of a woman's underclothing (such as a girdle) may be necessary if it is tight.

✖ **Never attempt to remove clothing** unless it is absolutely essential: much harm can be done by unnecessary attempts to do so.

Removing coats, jackets, shirts and vests

1 Raise the victim and slip the garment over the shoulders (**a**; see overleaf). **2** Bend the arm on the victim's uninjured side and remove the garment.

3 Gently slip out the other arm (**b**; see overleaf).

♦ **If removal is proving difficult**, then slitting the seam of the garment along the injured side may be helpful.

Removing coats, jackets, shirts and vests

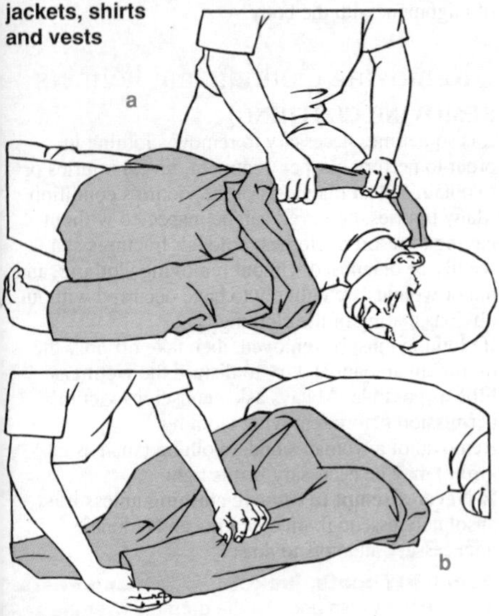

Trousers

1 Raise the trouser leg if the calf or knee is injured (**a**).

2 Pull the trousers down from the waist if the thigh is injured (**b**).

◆ **If removal is proving difficult**, then the first aider should slit the inner seam of the trouser leg.

Trousers

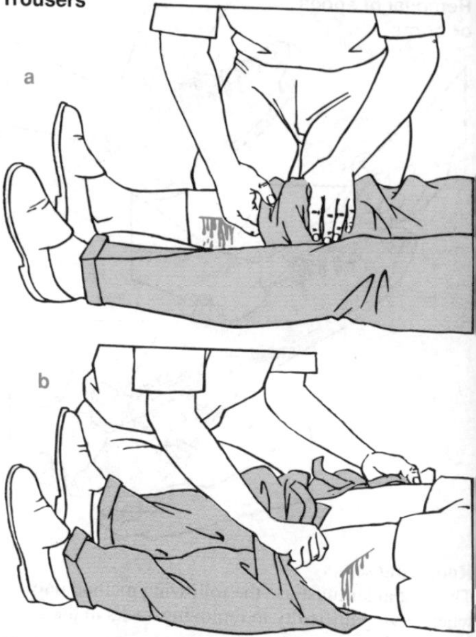

Removing shoes or boots (see overleaf)
1 Steady the victim's ankle (**a**). **2** Cut or undo any laces (**b**). **3** Remove the shoe (**c**).

♦ **If there is difficulty** in removing long boots, then carefully slit them up the back seam with a razor blade or sharp knife.

Removal of shoes or boots

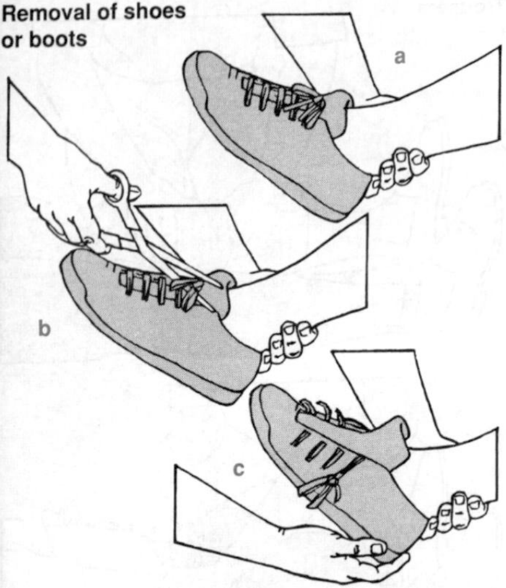

Removing socks

The first aider must use the following method only when having difficulty in removing socks in the ordinary way.

Method

1 Two fingers must be inserted between the sock and the victim's leg. **2** The edge of the sock must be raised and then cut between the first aider's fingers.

Removing socks

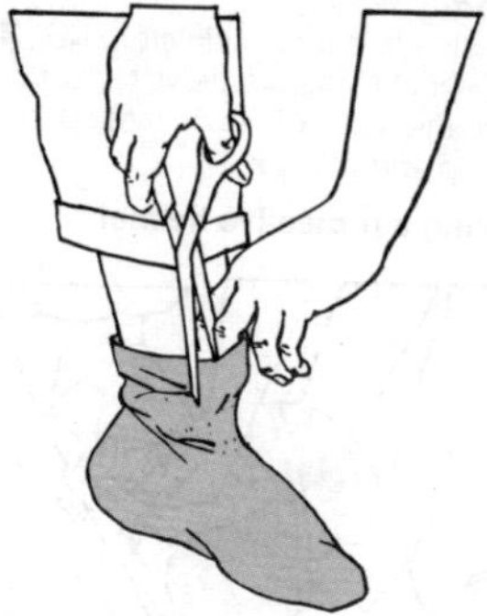

REMOVING HELMETS

The removal of two types of helmet – protective helmets and full-face crash helmets – is described here. First aiders are, in general, strongly advised not to try to remove a helmet, as such an action may – in the event of a neck fracture – cause paralysis or even death. In most cases, severe head injuries are actually prevented by crash helmets. If a helmet (of whatever type) has to be removed, remember the following points:

- take off any spectacles or sunglasses before removal;
- it is always best if the victim can remove the helmet him- or herself, if possible.

Removing a protective helmet

A protective helmet is here defined as that type which only covers the wearer's head. ▶ ▶

Method
1 Unfasten or cut the chin strap (**a**). **2** A second person should support the victim's head and neck. **3** Force the sides of the helmet apart. **4** Lift the helmet up and back (**b**).

Removing a protective helmet

a

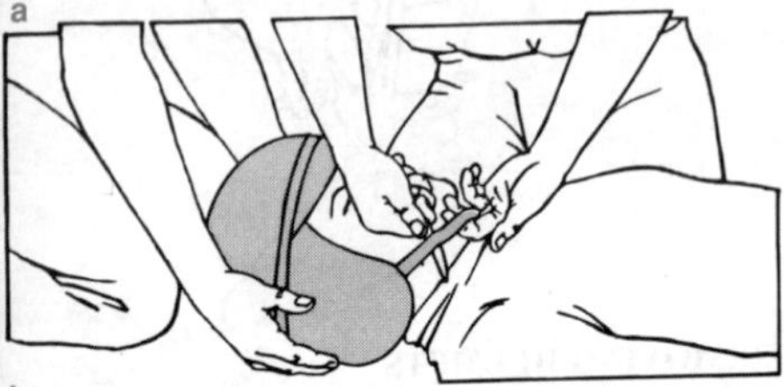

b

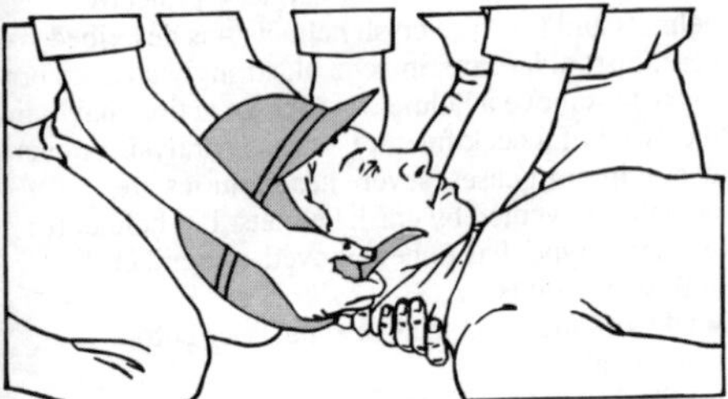

Removing a full-face crash helmet
Two people are required for this operation: one to support the victim's neck and head; the other to remove the helmet.

✖ **A full-face crash helmet should never** be removed unless it is a matter of life and death. Remove the helmet only if

- the victim's breathing is hampered by the helmet;
- the victim is not breathing and has no pulse;
- the victim is vomiting.

Method

1 Place your hands on each side of the helmet. Keep the head steady by placing your fingers on the victim's jaw. **2** A second person should cut or loosen the chin strap (**a**). **3** He or she should then support the victim's head by holding it at the base of the skull and the top of the neck. The chin should be held between the fingers and thumb of the other hand (**b**). **4** Tilt the helmet back to clear the chin and nose (**c**). **5** Tilt it forward to clear the base of the victim's skull (**d**). **6** Lift off the helmet (**e**).

Removing a full-face crash helmet

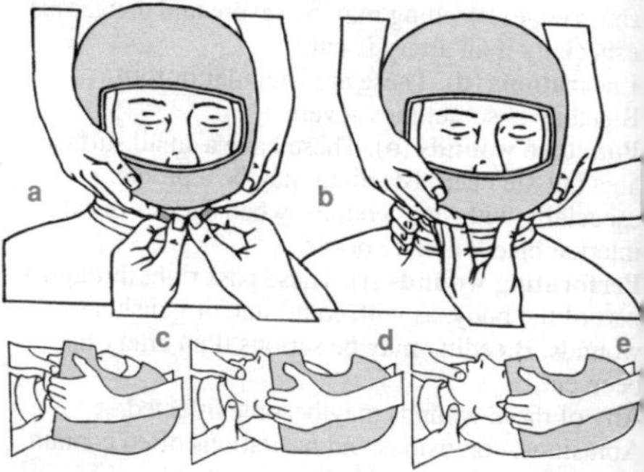

3. Major injuries and dangerous conditions

Bleeding

WOUNDS AND EXTERNAL BLEEDING

Minor wounds

See pp. 194–6 for the treatment and management of minor wounds.

Abrasions (a). These are on the surface only and are caused by a grazing or scraping. Bleeding is minimal.

Contusions (b). These are on and just under the surface, with skin splitting and bruising. Bleeding is seldom severe.

Major wounds

Incised wounds (c). These are cleanly cut by a sharp edge. Bleeding may be severe and dangerous, especially if an artery is cut.

Lacerations (d). These are irregular or torn. Bleeding is sometimes severe.

Puncture wounds (e). These have a small surface area but are deep. Bleeding may be a problem especially with stab wounds, when serious or fatal internal bleeding may occur.

Perforating wounds (f). These pass right through a part of the body, as with some stab or gunshot wounds. Bleeding may be serious if an artery has been cut.

Any of these wounds may become infected. Abrasions, contusions and lacerations often contain visible dirt. Puncture wounds can sometimes lead to dangerous infections, such as lockjaw (tetanus) or gas gangrene.

Types of wound

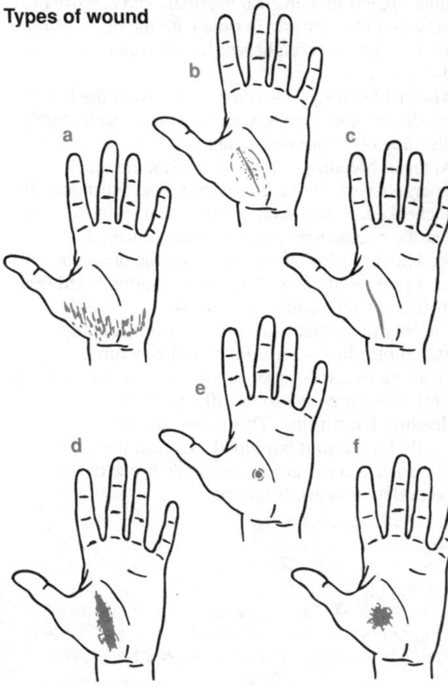

Blood loss and its control

The whole body contains about 5 litres (9 pints) of blood. If an artery is cut, the blood is pumped out under pressure with each heartbeat and can usually be seen to be spurting in time with the pulse. Blood from an artery is bright red; blood from a vein is a dull purplish colour.

Minor bleeding. This often comes from the blood capillaries and is usually an ooze or a trickle. Such bleeding offers no significant risk.

Arterial bleeding. This is one of the few real emergencies with which the first aider must deal. If unchecked, it may soon lead to so much blood loss that the circulation cannot be maintained (shock, see pp. 112–15), also fatally depriving the brain and heart muscle of blood. Torn arteries often bleed less profusely than cleanly cut vessels.

The only thing that takes priority over stopping arterial bleeding is ensuring that the victim is breathing freely. As soon as you see arterial bleeding apply direct pressure to the affected part.

Bleeding from veins. This is not pulsatile and is usually less serious but blood can gush if a large vein, such as a major varicose vein or one of the main internal veins, is injured.

Controlling bleeding

1 Apply direct pressure to the wound, using your fingers or hand (**a**). **2** If the wound is large, press the edges together, gently and firmly maintaining pressure (**b**). **3** Consider what you can use as a pad to control the bleeding more effectively. A clean folded handkerchief is often ideal. **4** If bleeding is from a limb, elevate it (**c**). Be careful if there is a possibility of a fracture (see pp. 129–31). **5** If direct pressure seems to be controlling the bleeding and you have a first aid kit, put a sterile or clean dressing (see pp.226–8) on the wound, covering it completely. ►►

Controlling bleeding

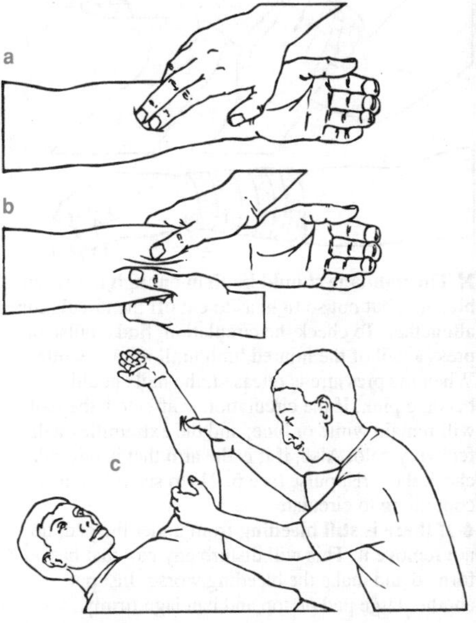

6 Apply a pad (see pp. 227–8) that covers the area of the wound. Press it down firmly (**d**). **7** Bandage it securely in place (**e**).

Controlling bleeding
(continued)

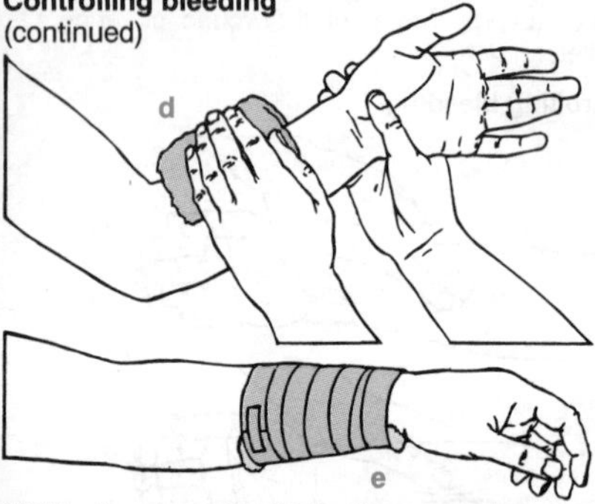

✖ **The bandage should be firm enough** to prevent bleeding but not so tight as to cut off the circulation altogether. To check the circulation, find a pulse or press a nail of the injured limb until it turns white. When the pressure is released, the nail should become pink. If the circulation is affected, the nail will remain white or blue; and the extremities will feel very cold. Also, if it is the arm that is injured, check the wrist pulse (see p. 21) to see if blood is continuing to circulate.

◆ **If there is still bleeding** from under the pad, do not remove it. This will disturb any clot that has formed and make the bleeding worse. Just put another large pad on top and bandage firmly.

♦ **If the bleeding still will not stop** using direct pressure or bandaging, you will have to use pressure on the artery leading to the wound (see 'Severe bleeding and pressure points', pp. 34–5).

Foreign bodies in wounds

Although dirt and other loose small-particle foreign material should be carefully washed out of minor wounds, larger foreign bodies should be left alone.

✖ **Never** try to prise foreign bodies out of deep wounds. This may precipitate severe bleeding.

Managing wounds with foreign bodies

Control bleeding and, if bleeding is not severe, dress the wound as for an open fracture (see pp. 132–3).

INTERNAL BLEEDING

This is often difficult to detect, but should be suspected when injuries are severe, as in road traffic accidents or a thigh fracture.

Features

- Bleeding from an orifice, such as the mouth, nose or ears.
- Growing swelling and tension.
- Extensive bruising.
- Restlessness.
- Signs of shock (see p. 113).

In the event of internal bleeding

1 Telephone for an ambulance immediately. The need to get the victim to hospital is very great.
2 Check and record the pulse rate every 5 minutes.
3 Treat for shock (see pp. 114–15).

Breathing difficulties

Minor breathing difficulty, such as mild asthma, will not require first aid but, unless the cause is known, medical advice should always be sought. Severe breathing difficulty is highly dangerous and calls for immediate remedial action. Airway obstruction (see pp. 19–20) is one of the most serious emergencies and it is one in which knowledgeable first aid, effectively applied, can often save a life.

ASPHYXIA

Asphyxia is lack of oxygen in the blood. It is caused by the interruption of the free flow of air into and out of the tiny air sacs in the lungs. This is usually the cause of death in choking (opposite), drowning (see pp. 83–4), strangulation (see p. 87), inhalation of a gas or fumes which exclude oxygen (see pp. 85–6), foreign body airway obstruction (see pp. 19–20) and swelling of the soft tissues of the voice box (oedema of the larynx) (see p. 100).

If asphyxia is being caused by any external agency, such as a plastic bag or a pillow, this should, of course, be removed at once and the breathing (see pp. 17–18) and pulse (see p. 21) checked.

Appropriate resuscitation, if necessary, should immediately be undertaken (see pp. 22–9).

CHOKING

Choking is commonly caused by the inhalation of a foreign body, such as a lump of ill-chewed food or a hard toffee, into the voice box (larynx) or major air passages (**a**). This can happen if a person is laughing or starts to sneeze while eating. Airway obstruction of this kind cannot be helped by mouth-to-mouth ventilation – which might, indeed, make matters worse. The urgent necessity is to get rid of the obstruction, after which artificial ventilation (see pp. 23–4) may be supplied, if necessary.

Features

The victim

- grasps her throat (a highly characteristic sign) (**b**);
- shows marked indications of distress and panic;
- is unable to talk;
- may first breathe noisily then not at all;
- turns blue or sometimes grey or pale;
- becomes unconscious within a minute or so.

Choking

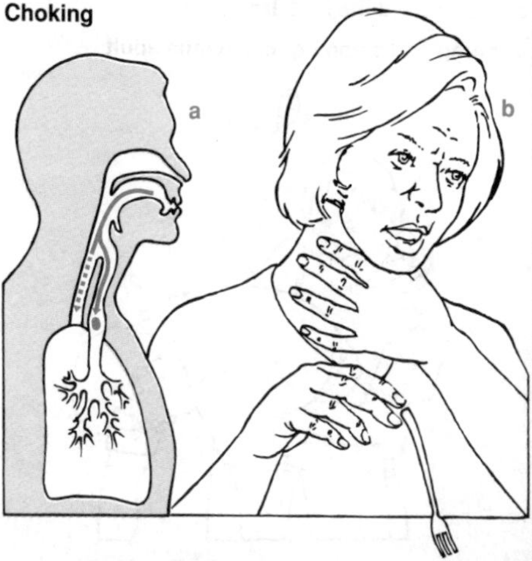

Coughing up the obstruction

Conscious adult and child. 1 If the victim is an adult, ask him or her if choking is occurring. **2** If air can be inhaled, encourage strong coughing after slow inhalation. Violent inhalation may make matters worse.

♦ **If this fails**, the following should be attempted.

Bending and slapping

Conscious adult. 1 The victim should bend over so that the head is lower than the lungs. **2** Slap him sharply between the shoulder blades with the heel of the hand.

Do not be afraid of hurting him. This is a dire emergency and life is in danger.

Bending and slapping: conscious adult

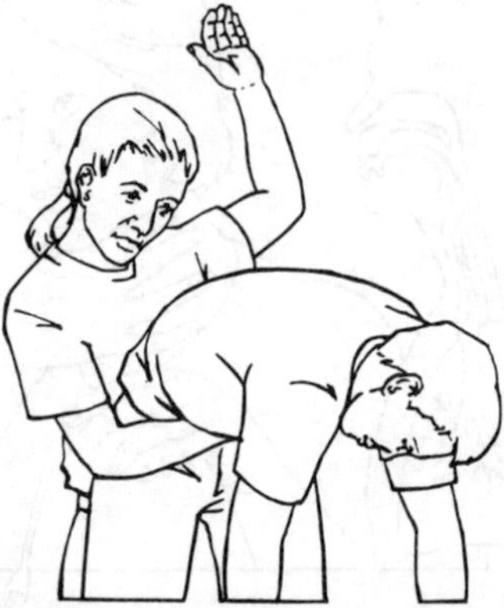

Conscious child. Rest him, face down, on your knees and try slapping between the shoulder blades with the heel of the hand. Try this four times if necessary.

Bending and slapping: conscious child

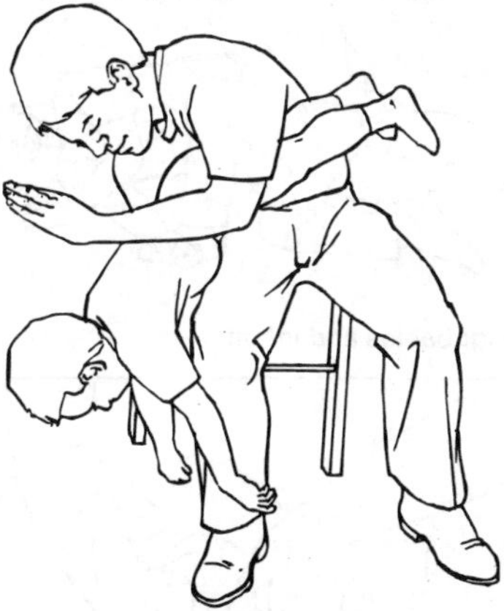

Unconscious adult and child. 1 Turn the victim onto the side closest to you. **2** Push the head back. **3** Slap the back four times, if necessary, with the heel of your hand.

Babies and infants. 1 The infant should be supported, face down, on the forearm. **2** The head and chest should be supported by the hand. **3** Give the infant four smart slaps between the shoulder blades with your fingers. ►►

Slapping: unconscious adult and child

Slapping: babies and infants

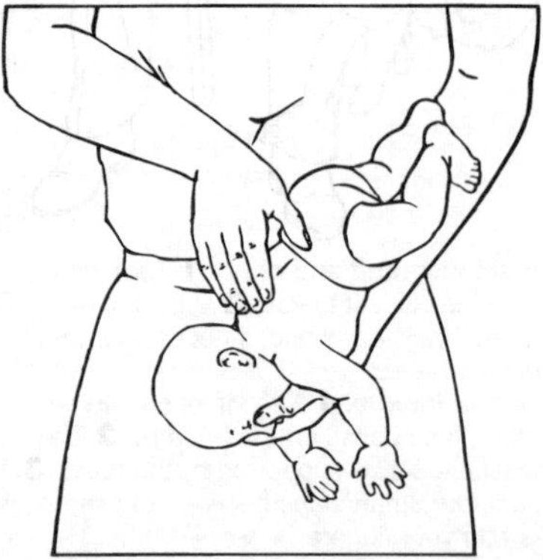

♦ **If this fails**, use the abdominal thrust method.

The abdominal thrust method

This can be used either on a conscious or an unconscious victim of choking. The abdominal thrust should cause a sudden rise in pressure in the lungs, driving out the obstruction like a cork from a champagne bottle.

✖ **This should not be tried** unless coughing, and bending and slapping have failed, as it may cause internal injury. Do not, however, omit it on this account, for if there is complete airway obstruction, the victim will quickly die unless it is relieved.

Using the abdominal thrust

Conscious adult. 1 Stand behind him, put one arm around him, clench your fist and place it in the middle of the abdomen, between the nâvel and the lower angle of the ribs (**a**). ►►

Abdominal thrust: conscious adult

a

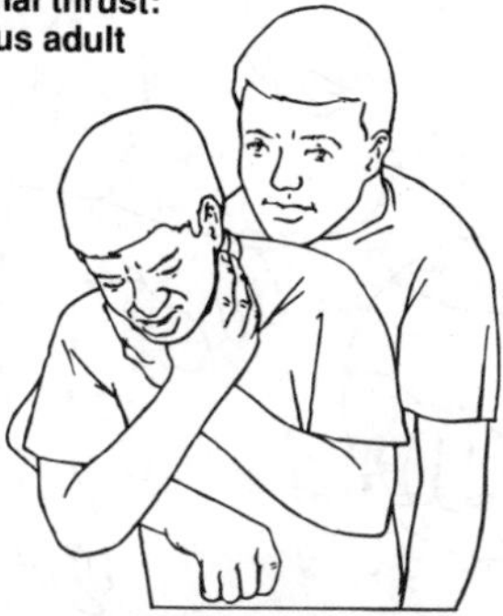

2 Turn the thumb inwards. **3** Grasp your fist with the other hand (**b**) and pull both firmly against the victim's body (**c**). **4** Suddenly, thrust inwards and upwards with considerable force so as to compress the upper abdomen and push upwards on the diaphragm – the muscular sheet that is the flexible floor of the chest. **5** Repeat up to four times, if necessary.

Abdominal thrust: conscious adult
(continued)

Conscious child. 1 Take the child on your knee. **2** Thrust with one fist only, using counter-pressure on the back with the other hand.

Abdominal thrust: conscious child

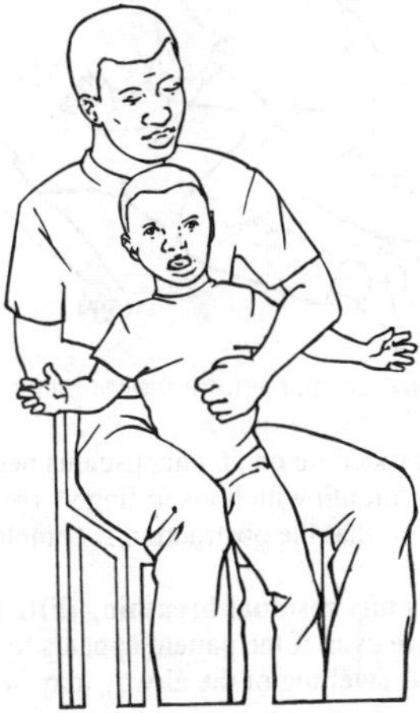

Unconscious adult. 1 Turn her on her back with the chin up and the head tilted back. **2** Kneel alongside or, preferably, astride the upper thighs, facing the head. **3** Put the heel of one hand on the midline of the upper abdomen, between the navel and the rib angle, and cover it with your other hand. Thrust forcibly inwards and upwards. **4** Repeat up to four times. ►►

Abdominal thrust: unconscious adult

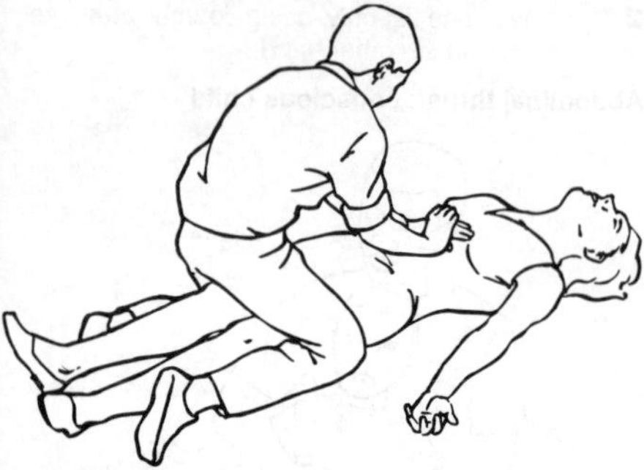

Unconscious child. Perform the thrust as with adults but using one hand only.

After each procedure on an unconscious person, clear out the mouth with hooked fingers (see pp. 19–20), so that the obstruction is completely removed.

◆ **If there is any residual breathing difficulty**, call an ambulance even if the patient appears to have recovered, as swelling of the airway may occur.

DROWNING

Never assume that a person has drowned even if she has been under water for many minutes. People have recovered fully after immersion in cold water for half an hour. This is possible as body cooling slows metabolic processes and the brain can survive the lack of oxygen for longer than normal.

The first aider should take into account any possible dangers that they may encounter when trying to rescue a drowning person.

Resuscitating a drowning person

1 While removing the person from the water, apply mouth-to-mouth ventilation (**a**). In between breaths, move to dry land. ►►

Resuscitating a drowning person

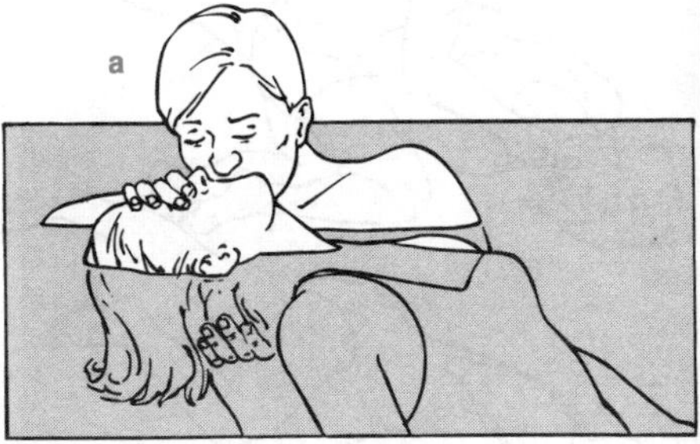

2 Get the person out of the water as quickly as possible. **3** Check breathing (see pp. 17–18). **4** Check the pulse (see p. 21). **5** If artifical ventilation is still needed, turn the victim's head to the side and clear the mouth of any material (**b**) (see pp. 19–20). Also, the victim will bring up water. **6** If the victim is breathing, put her into the recovery position (**c**) (see pp. 31–3). **7** If the victim is breathing but is very cold, treat for hypothermia (see pp. 127–8). **8** Get the victim to hospital as soon as possible.

Resuscitating a drowning person (continued)

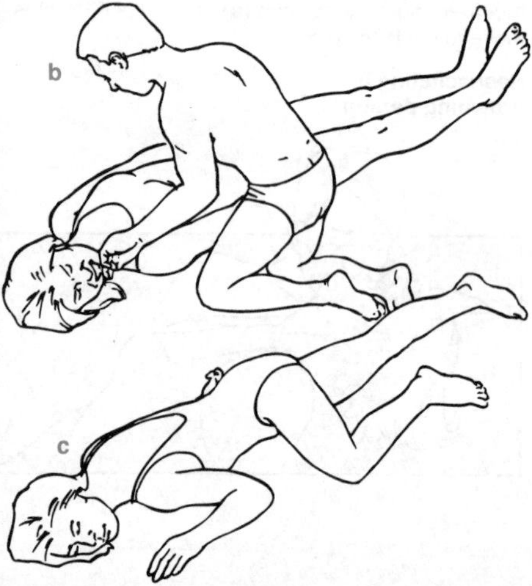

FUMES AND GASES

Carbon monoxide poisoning

This is a colourless, odourless, tasteless and poisonous gas, present in large quantity in the exhaust of motor vehicles. It is also produced by coal-burning fires or furnaces. Carbon monoxide combines readily with the haemoglobin of the blood, forming a stable compound (carboxyhaemoglobin) and cutting the ability of the red blood cells to carry oxygen. If half an adult's haemoglobin becomes carboxyhaemoglobin, this may lead to death. Rapid rescue of a person, e.g. from a closed garage, is unlikely to be dangerous, especially if doors and windows are opened.

Once the victim is in the open air

1 Check for breathing (**a**) (see pp. 17–18). **2** Check the pulse (see p. 21). **3** Perform resuscitation if needed (see pp. 22–9). **4** Put the victim into the recovery position (**b**) (see pp. 31–3). **5** Arrange for removal to hospital.

Carbon monoxide poisoning

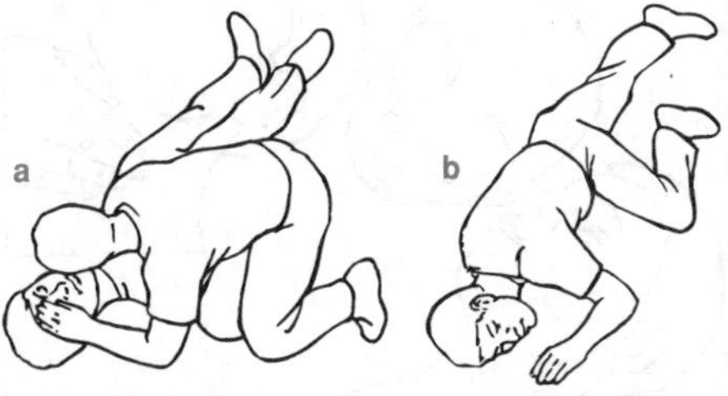

Smoke inhalation

The fire that causes smoke will reduce the local available oxygen, leading to asphyxia. Smoke is often highly irritating to the airway and may even cause tight closure of the vocal cords, so cutting off the airway. Some types of smoke are very poisonous. You will need to decide whether to risk attempting an immediate removal of the victim, or victims, from the fire or whether first to call the fire and ambulance services.

Once the victim has been dragged away from the smoke and their burning clothes have been dealt with (see p. 91), take the following measures.

In the event of smoke inhalation

1 Check the airway, breathing (see pp. 17–18) (**a**) and pulse (see p. 21) (**b**). **2** Perform artificial ventilation if necessary (see pp. 23–4). **3** Check for burns and treat appropriately (see pp. 92, 94 and 208). **4** Arrange for removal to hospital.

Smoke inhalation

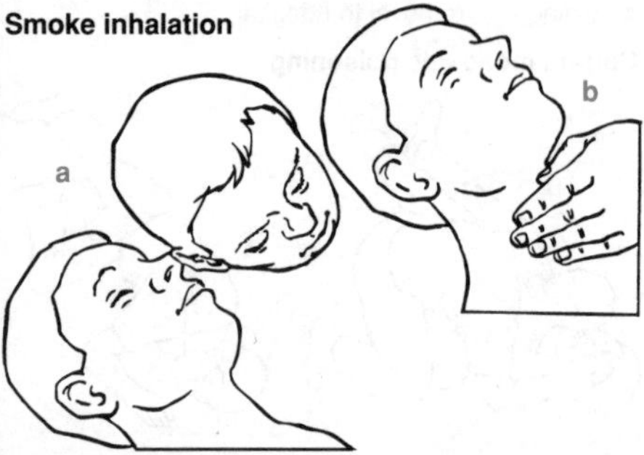

STRANGULATION

Unconsciousness or death may result from compression of the arteries in the neck as well as from interference with the airway. There may also be spinal injury.

In the event of strangulation

1 Relieve the constriction around the neck by lifting up and supporting the victim (**a**), so that the weight can be taken off the neck. **2** Cut the ligature beneath the knot (**b**). **3** Check for breathing (see pp. 17–18). **4** Check the pulse (see p. 21).
5 Perform resuscitation, if needed (see pp. 22–9).
6 Place in the recovery position, if necessary.
7 Arrange for transport to hospital.

If there is any suggestion of foul play, contact the police; tell them what you found and did.

Strangulation

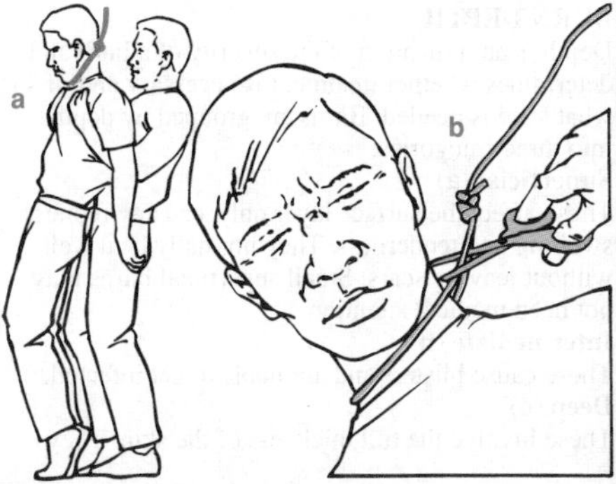

Burns

CAUSES

Burns are tissue injuries caused by

- high or very low temperatures;
- radiation: sunlight and other ultraviolet sources, X- rays, gamma rays;
- corrosive chemicals;
- electrical current flowing through the body – this has a heating and coagulating effect and may interfere with breathing and the heartbeat;
- friction.

Tissue is liable to be destroyed if the causal agent is allowed to continue to act. First aid thus consists, if possible, of reducing (or raising) temperature, removing the victim from the source of radiation, or removing the injurious chemical by brushing and/or washing.

BURN DEPTH

Depth is an indication of the severity of a burn and determines whether treatment is necessary and, if so, what kind is needed. Burns are grouped by depth into three categories.

Superficial (a)

These affect the surface layer only, causing redness, swelling and tenderness. They normally heal well without leaving scars. Small superficial burns may not need medical attention.

Intermediate (b)

These cause blisters and are liable to get infected.

Deep (c)

These involve the full thickness of the skin. They

appear grey, waxy-looking or charred, and may be painless, even if large, because the nerves may have been destroyed. Large burns will usually be in the deep category.

Burn depth

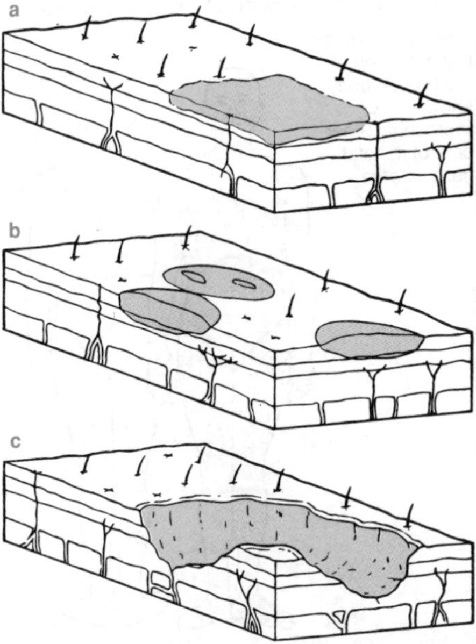

BURN AREA

The larger the area of the burn, the more serious it is likely to be. Even superficial burns can be dangerous if very large. Burns over 3 cm across should be seen by a doctor. In large burns, an assessment of the danger is made using the 'rule of nines'. Any person with a burn, even a superficial burn, of more than

The rule of nines
Each division of the human body, shown here, represents 9 per cent of its total surface area.

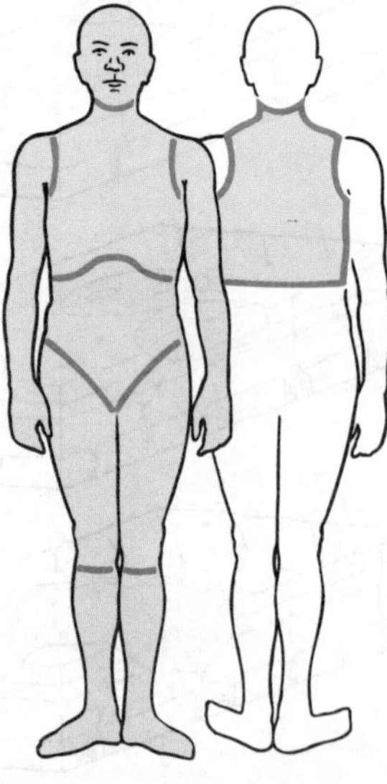

9 per cent of the body area, will require hospital attention. Surgical shock (see pp. 112–15) and infection are the main risks to life from extensive burns; the rule of nines is an important way of assessing the danger and determining the need for blood or other transfusions. After the first 48 hours, the main danger is from infection.

CLOTHING ON FIRE

Many serious burns are caused by clothing, especially loose, light clothing like nightgowns, catching fire. Fire starting at the hem often spreads rapidly upwards by convection, if the person concerned remains standing or runs about.

If clothing is on fire

1 Make the victim lie down at once. **2** Use a dry powder extinguisher if you have one, or try to smother the flames with any suitable heavy material. This will exclude oxygen. If no smothering materials are to hand lie the victim's burning side on the ground to extinguish the flames.

Clothing on fire

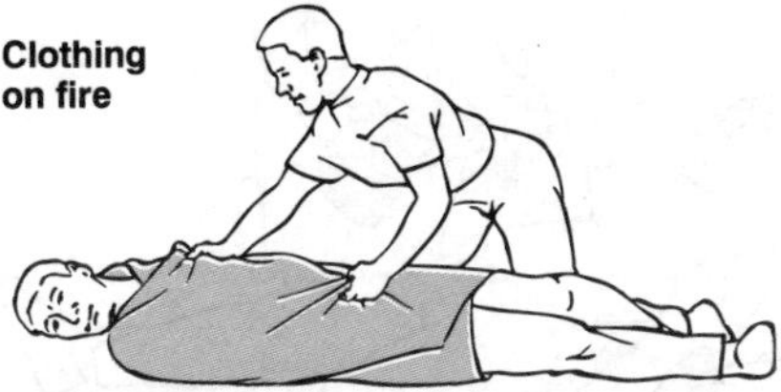

✖ **Do not use nylon.**

✖ **Do not roll** the person along the ground as this may extend the burned area. ►►

Once the flames are out

Rapid cooling is the next priority. Do not waste any time.

Rapid cooling and preventing infection

1 Hot clothing can cause serious burns, so remove or cut them off or cool with water. **2** Cool the victim for the next 10 minutes by pouring buckets and jugs of cold water over him (**a**). **3** Telephone for an ambulance. **4** Check that the airway is clear (see pp. 19–20). **5** Cover the burns (**b**, **c**) with clean dressings to reduce the risk of infection. **6** Give the victim regular sips of cold water, if conscious, to replace any lost fluid.

Rapid cooling and preventing infection

a

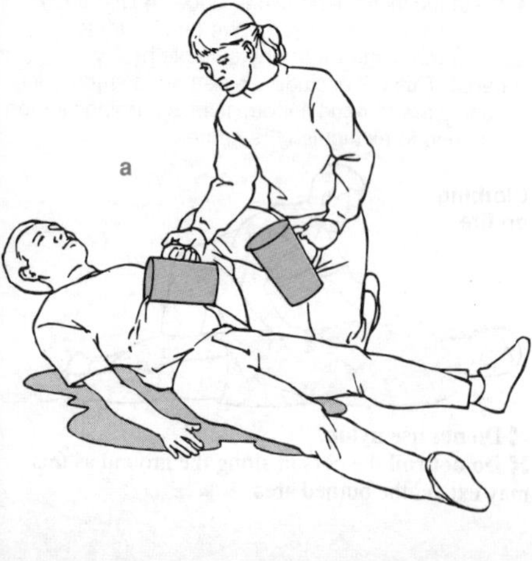

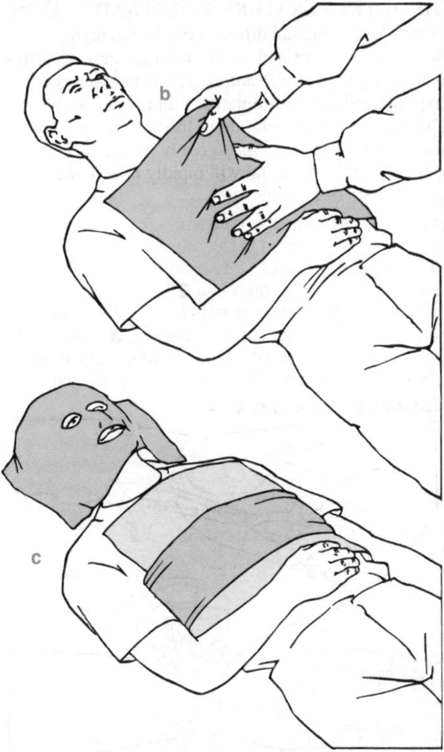
b
c

HIGH-TEMPERATURE BURNS AND SCALDS

There is no essential difference between high-temperature burns and scalds; both are tissue injuries caused by high temperatures. Tissue damage occurs rapidly, and the most important thing that can be done is for the temperature of the burn to be reduced immediately. Cooling may greatly reduce the severity of the burn and will rapidly relieve the severe pain of burning.

Treating burns and scalds

See p. 208 for minor burns and scalds.

1 Remove or cut away any clothes that are covering the burned area (**a**). **2** Remove any potentially constricting objects (rings, bracelets, watches, etc.) before swelling occurs. **3** Hold the burned part under a cold tap, a garden hose or a cold shower, and run the water on it for at least

Treating burns and scalds

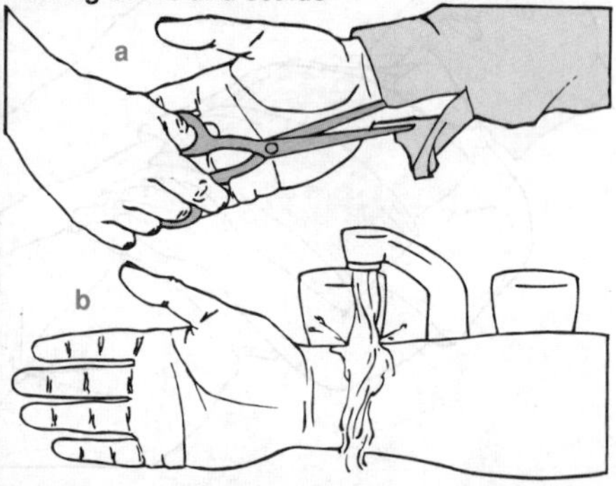

10 minutes (**b**). This measure alone can make the difference between a serious and a trivial burn and should be used, if possible, for all burns.

✘ **Do not apply** butter, ointments or lotions.

✘ **Do not pull** off anything that is stuck to a burn.

Blisters

These should be kept intact if at all possible. Blisters may be protected by careful padding with loose cotton wool fixed, without undue pressure, using clear sticky tape.

Dressing broken blisters

1 Broken blisters should be covered with sterile dressings (**a**), if available. **2** Add extra padding using cotton wool secured with clear sticky tape (**b**).

✘ **Do not deliberately cut or prick** a blister. The outer layer of skin forms an ideal dressing over the raw tissue underneath, which is very susceptible to infection.

Dressing broken blisters

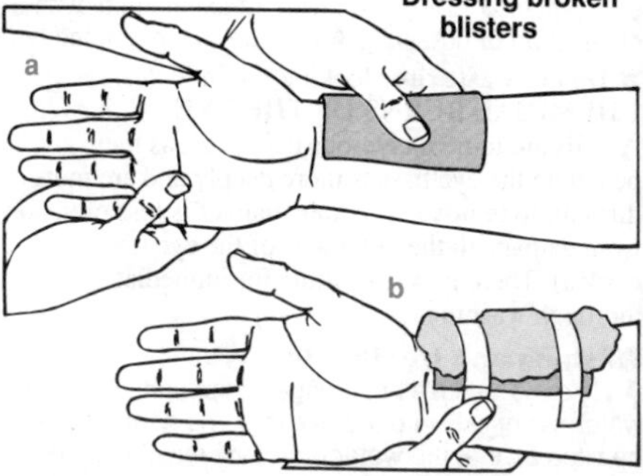

CHEMICAL BURNS

These are mainly caused by strong acids from car batteries, or alkalis such as caustic soda or strong bleach. Paint strippers and some household cleansers are also corrosive. Take care, in dealing with these situations, not to come into contact with the chemical.

Features

- Stinging sensation of the skin.
- Rapid staining and discolouration.
- Reddening, blistering or peeling.

Treating a chemical burn

1 Immediately and thoroughly wash the affected area under a hose or tap. This will remove surplus material, dilute the chemical and reduce the severity of the burn. If a dry chemical is involved, brush it off with a soft brush first. **2** While washing, remove or cut off any clothing contaminated by the corrosive substance. **3** Cover the burn, if it is inflamed, with a clean cloth or dressing. **4** Get the victim to hospital.

✗ **Do not waste time** looking for antidotes.

CHEMICAL BURNS OF THE EYE

Alkalis are more dangerous than acids as they penetrate the eye tissues more deeply and are more difficult to remove. The main danger is loss of vision from damage to the outer lens of the eye (the cornea). There is no substitute for immediate, thorough washing.

Washing and treating the eye

1 Hold the victim's head under a tap and let the water run briskly into the eye (**a**). The head should be tilted so that the water runs past the side of the head and not into the undamaged eye. **2** It is essential that the lids should be kept separated during the washing. If the victim cannot do this voluntarily, the lids must be held open (**b**). **3** Maintain the washing for as long as reasonably possible. Ten minutes is not too long for an alkali burn. If both eyes are affected, wash them alternately for 10 seconds each. **4** After irrigation, apply a sterile or clean pad over the closed eye and fix with clear sticky tape (**c**). **5** Take the victim to hospital as soon as possible for ophthalmic attention.

♦ **If a tap is not available**, any bland fluid, such as beer, milk or, if all else fails, urine can be used. Urine is usually sterile and is harmless.

Washing and treating the eye

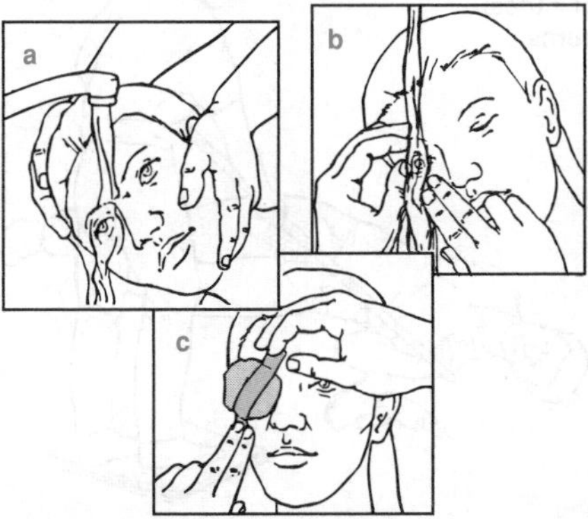

ELECTRICAL BURNS

The first priority is to break the contact between the victim and the electricity supply, without electrocuting yourself.

In the event of electric shock and burns

1 Switch off the current, wrench out the flex or pull out the plug immediately. Switch the electricity off at the mains if this is quicker. **2** If necessary, use a broom handle or a wooden chair, while standing on a dry rubber mat, book or folded newspaper, to move the victim's limb from the point of electrical contact (**a**). **3** When safe, check the victim's breathing and heartbeat. **4** Attempt artificial ventilation and

Electrical burns

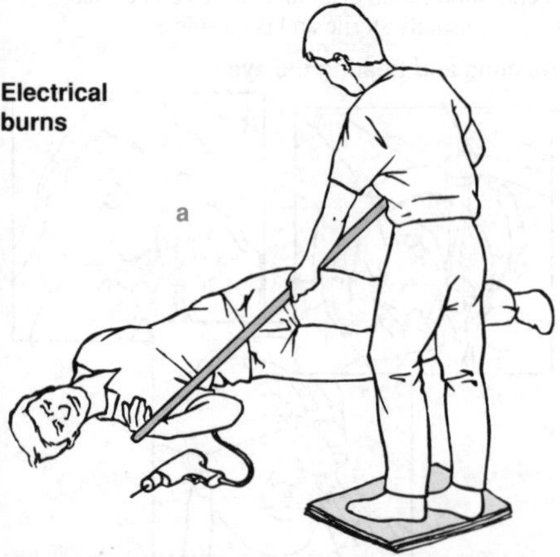

external chest compression (see pp. 23–4 and 26–8), if necessary. **5** Place the victim in the recovery position, if unconscious. **6** Treat the burns, at the points where the electricity entered and left the body, by cooling them with water. **7** Apply a sterile or clean pad and a bandage (**b**).

b

✖ **Never apply water** while the victim is still connected to the electricity supply.

High-voltage electricity

Contact with high-voltage electricity, e.g. from an overhead power line, is usually fatal to the victim. You, too, could be killed by 'arcing' or jumping electricity, if you are 18 metres (20 yards) or less from the source. Keep other people away and call the police immediately.

MOUTH AND THROAT BURNS

The immediate danger here is to the airway from swelling of the soft tissues of the voice box (larynx) leading to possible asphyxia.

Causes

- Accidentally drinking scalding liquids.
- Drinking corrosive poisons.
- Inhaling hot air, steam or gases.

Treating mouth and throat burns

1 Telephone for an ambulance at once. **2** Relieve any constriction on the outside of the neck (**a**). **3** Reassure the victim. **4** Give regular sips of cold water (**b**). Giving the victim ice cubes or ice cream to suck will be highly effective, too.

◆ **If consciousness is lost**, put the victim into the recovery position (see pp. 31–3) and check the airway (see pp. 17–19). Use resuscitation if necessary. Get the victim to hospital as quickly as possible.

Mouth and throat burns

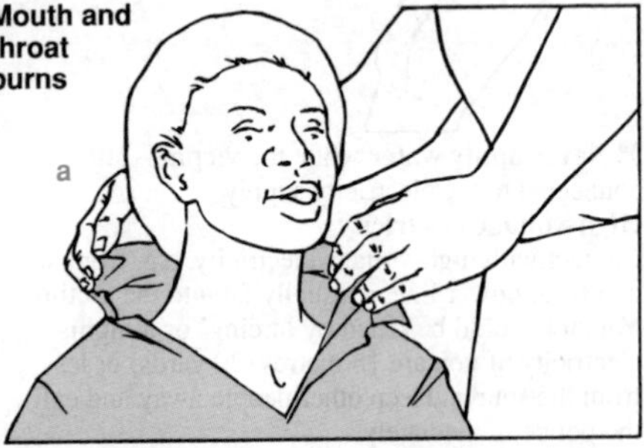

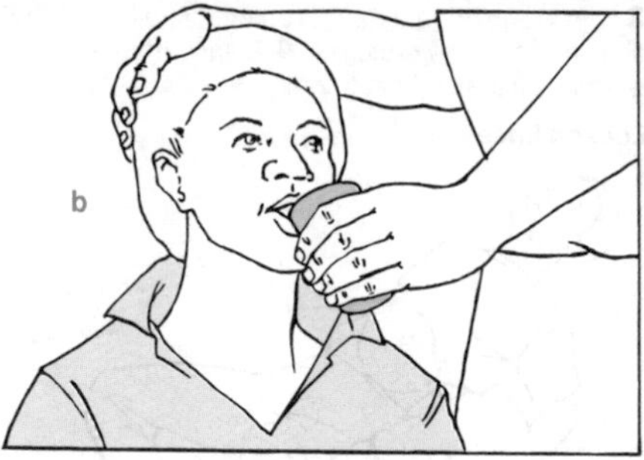

Cartilage injuries

LOCKED KNEE

This is a result of a tear and displacement of one of the half-moon cartilages inside the knee joint. This is a common sports injury usually caused by a twisting strain when the knee is fully straight. The torn cartilage slips from its usual position between the bearing surfaces of the joint, preventing their normal movement.

Features

- Pain.
- Sometimes a popping sound as the cartilage tears.
- Swelling.
- Inability to bend or straighten the knee.

✖ **Do not try** to bend or straighten the injured knee.

Treating locked knee

1 Apply a cold pack – ice or frozen peas. **2** Give the victim painkillers, such as aspirin or ibuprofen. ►►

3 The victim should be moved on a stretcher or he should use elbow crutches. **4** Transport to a hospital casualty department.

Locked knee

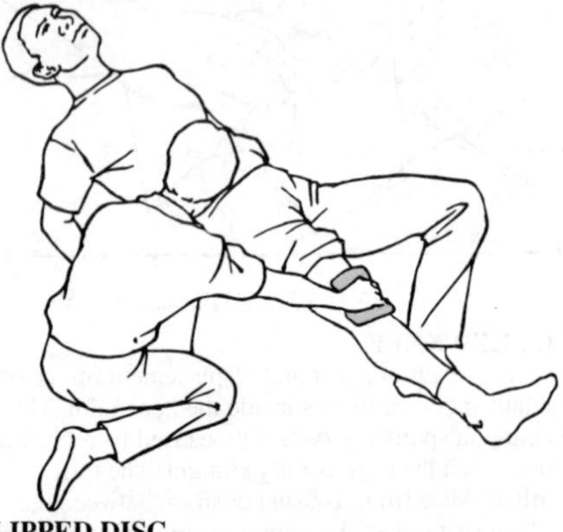

SLIPPED DISC

This is a misleading term. The disc (**a**) concerned lies between adjacent bones of the spine (vertebrae) (**b**) and is so securely fixed that it cannot slip. What happens is that some of the pulpy interior of the disc gets squeezed out through a tear in the strong outer fibrous ring of the disc. This pulpy material (**c**) can press on the nerves (**d**) emerging from the spinal cord. The problem usually affects a disc in the lower back and the nerves concerned are those joining to form the sciatic nerve of the leg.

Features

- Low back pain or, less commonly, neck pain.
- There may be pain in the buttock or down the back of the leg.
- Spasm of the muscles of the lower back or neck.
- There may be numbness in the leg or foot.

When a slipped disc is suspected

1 The victim should lie down on a firm surface, such as a mattress on the floor, and find the most comfortable position. Ideally, the shoulders, hips and ankles should all be level with each other (**e**).

2 Give painkillers such as aspirin or ibuprofen.

3 If symptoms persist, call a doctor. The length of time for which symptoms may persist depends on their severity.

Slipped disc

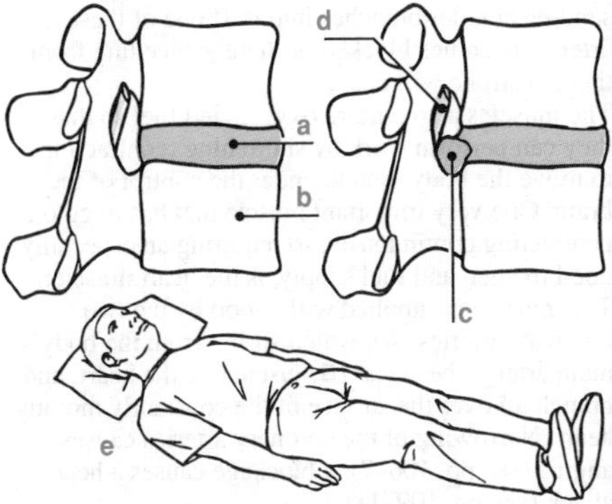

Circulatory problems

THE CIRCULATORY SYSTEM AND ITS FUNCTION

The brain is the most important organ in the body. The other organs are concerned with its support and maintenance. This is especially true of the heart, which is a muscular pump that keeps blood circulating to the lungs, to pick up oxygen, and to the intestines and liver to pick up fuel, which is mainly in the form of glucose. The essential thing is that blood containing plenty of oxygen and glucose should be continuously supplied to the brain. If this fails, death occurs quickly. So the brain normally has a very good blood supply provided by four large arteries that run up the neck. These branch repeatedly and run all over the surface of the brain sending smaller branches into it. If one of these arteries becomes blocked or there is bleeding from them, a stroke will occur.

The muscles also require oxygen and fuel so that they can perform work by shortening (contracting) to move the body around under the control of the brain. One very important muscle that has to go on contracting continuously, so requiring an especially good oxygen and fuel supply, is the heart muscle. This muscle is supplied with blood by the two coronary arteries (**A**), which spring from the body's main artery (the aorta) (**B**) just above the heart, and branch all over the surface of the constantly moving heart. Narrowing of the coronary arteries causes angina (see pp. 106–7); a blockage causes a heart attack (see pp. 109–11).

The heart pumps blood at high pressure into the arteries and receives it back at low pressure by way of the veins. The heart is divided in two (**C**), with right and left sides. The right side (from the person's own point of view) receives blood from the head and body, but not from the lungs, and pumps it to the lungs. Blood from the lungs returns to the left side of the heart which pumps it to the rest of the body. So the blood circulation resembles a 'figure-of-eight'. Blood in the arteries of the body (oxygenated blood) is bright red; blood in the veins (deoxygenated blood) is a dark purplish colour. The opposite holds for the lung circulation.

The heart

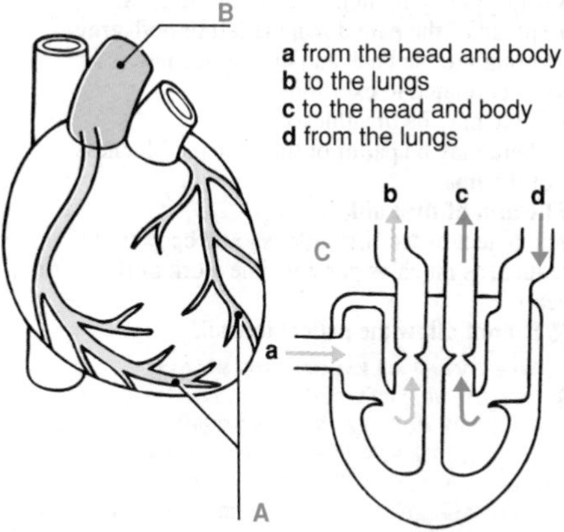

ANGINA

Angina pectoris is a symptom of heart disease, not a disease in itself. It is the pain that originates in the heart muscle when it is trying to perform work without getting enough blood, and hence oxygen and glucose. Blood is supplied to the heart muscle by way of the coronary arteries. If one of the branches of these arteries is severely narrowed by the disease atherosclerosis, it may not be able to carry enough blood to meet the requirements of the heart muscle. Angina is nearly always caused in this way, and nearly always occurs after a fixed amount of exertion or during strong emotional reactions.

Features

- A gripping pain in the centre of the chest.
- Spread of the pain down the left or both arms, through to the back and up into the jaw.
- Onset related to exertion.
- There may be breathlessness.
- There may be pallor of the skin and blueness of the lips.

The aim of first aid

The object of the first aider should be to try to reduce, as much as possible, the work of the victim's heart.

✘ **Do not allow** the patient to walk.

In the event of an angina attack

1 Help the victim to sit down and to assume the most comfortable position. Use rolled-up clothing for padding (**a**). **2** Ask if he has any angina medication (glyceryl-trinitrate) with him. If he does, and it is in pill form it should be placed under the tongue. If it is in spray form, it should be sprayed under the tongue. **3** Loosen tight clothing to ease breathing (**b**). **4** Reassure him. **5** Check that the pain passes within a minute or two of resting.

♦ **If the pain persists**, this is not angina but a heart attack (see pp. 109–11). Urgent removal to hospital is vital and may save life.

Angina attack

CARDIAC ARREST

Cardiac arrest means that the heart has stopped beating. This, of course, is very serious and will quickly result in death unless the heart can be restarted.

Features

- The victim collapses and quickly becomes unconscious and motionless.
- There are no breathing movements.
- The pulse cannot be felt anywhere.
- The skin is a grey colour.

In the event of cardiac arrest

1 Call for help. **2** Ask someone to telephone for an ambulance. He or she must say that the victim has had a cardiac arrest. **3** Perform two mouth-to-mouth inflations (**a**) (see p. 23). **4** Start external chest compression (**b**) (see pp. 26–8). **5** Give two inflations after every 15 compressions. Continue resuscitation until paramedical help arrives.

Cardiac arrest

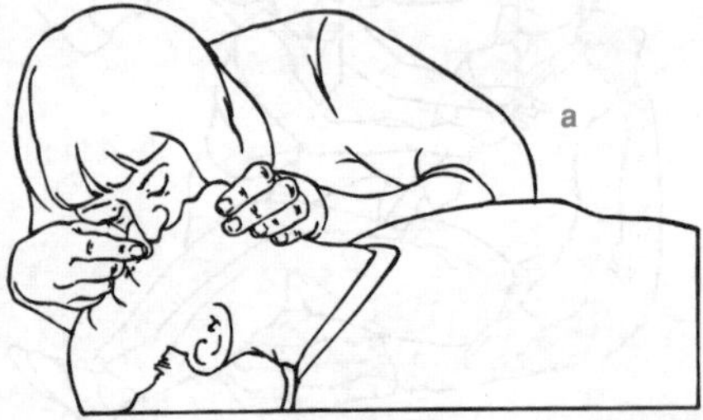

Cardiac arrest (continued)

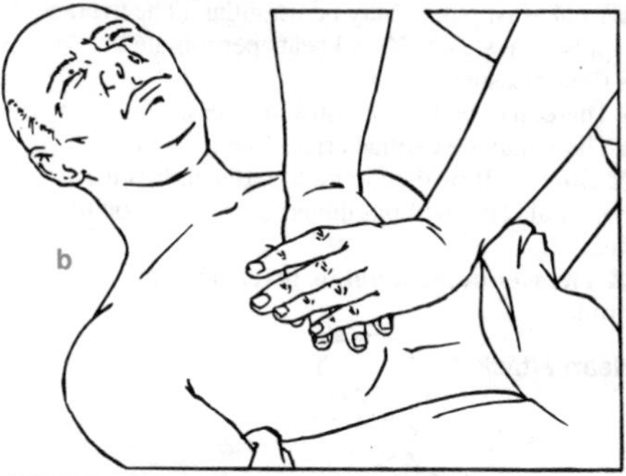

b

HEART ATTACK

This is caused by blockage of a branch of a coronary artery. The part of the heart muscle previously supplied by the blocked branch dies. If the area is large, the victim is unlikely to survive; but if it is small, recovery is possible. In that event, the dead area of muscle is replaced by scar tissue, so the power of the heart is weakened. Some people survive several heart attacks but their hearts may be seriously damaged.

Features

- Sudden onset of crushing central chest pain.
- Pain may spread to arms, back or throat (**a**; see overleaf).
- Conviction that one is dying.
- Faintness and falling.
- Profuse sweating.

- Pale skin.
- Weak, fast pulse. May be irregular. (The average pulse is a steady 60–80 beats per minute.)
- Breathlessness.
- There may be loss of consciousness.
- There may be cardiac arrest (see p. 108).

✖ **Do not allow** the victim to move unless it is essential. This will put unnecessary strain on the heart.

✖ **The victim must not be given** anything to eat or drink.

Heart attack

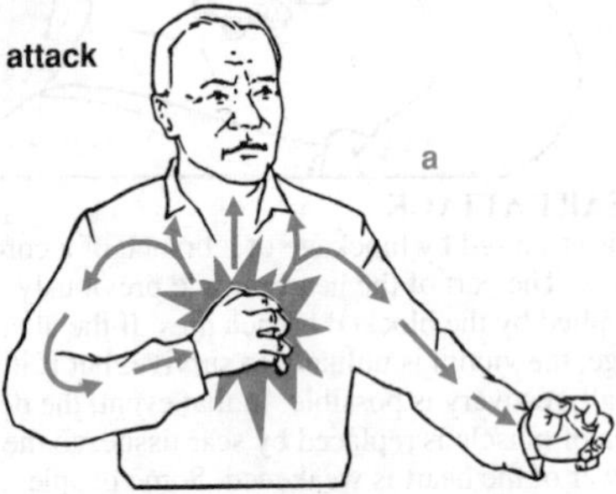

In the event of a heart attack

1 If the victim is conscious, manoeuvre him into a half-sitting position. The head, shoulders and knees should be supported by cushions (**b**). **2** Reassure the victim and help him to relax. **3** Call for help and ask someone to telephone for an ambulance. He or she must say that the victim has had a heart attack. **4** Loosen tight clothing at the neck, chest and waist (**c**).

5 Check for pulse (see p. 21) and breathing (see pp. 17–18). **6** If the victim becomes unconscious put him into the recovery position (see pp. 31–3) but maintain checks on breathing and pulse.
7 If breathing stops, use mouth-to-mouth ventilation (see pp. 23–4). **8** If heart stops, start chest compression (see pp. 26–8).

b

c

SHOCK

This term is not well understood outside medical circles because the same word is used for 'fright'. Surgical shock has nothing to do with fright. It is a condition in which either the amount of fluid in the blood vessels is insufficient to fill them or the heart output is not high enough to keep the blood circulating. In either case, the blood pressure drops and the supply of oxygen and fuel to the vital organs, especially the brain, heart and kidneys, is not enough to keep them working properly, if at all. The body does what it can to compensate, by shutting down the arteries to the less vital parts such as the skin and intestines, but there is a limit to this. Shock is very dangerous and, unless corrected, can rapidly prove fatal.

Causes

- Blood loss, whether external or internal, e.g. from spinal injury, into the tissues. Serious loss of blood, usually from an artery, may reduce the volume of the blood to the point where there is not enough to fill the blood vessels.
- Loss of fluid by prolonged vomiting or diarrhoea. This fluid has to come from the blood, which is reduced in volume.
- Burns. Large quantities of fluid may be lost from the surface or into blisters.
- Infection. Severe blood infection (septicaemia) may cause the blood vessels to widen and may lead to leakage of fluid from the blood into the tissues.
- Heart failure. If the heart muscle is weakened it may not be able to keep the blood circulating.

Features

- Pale and cold skin because the skin blood vessels are shut down.
- Rapid pulse because the heart is trying to maintain the circulation.
- Weak pulse because the heart cannot beat strongly.
- The victim feels faint and weak because of the reduced blood supply to the brain and the muscles.
- Severe breathlessness because the blood contains insufficient oxygen.
- Severe thirst because the fluid content of the blood is reduced.
- Possible loss of consciousness because of the reduced blood supply to the brain.

The aims of first aid

The aims of first aid are to try to prevent the worsening of shock and to make the best use of the limited available circulating blood.

✘ **Do not move** the victim unless it is essential. This could make the shock worse.

✘ **Do not give** the victim anything to eat or drink.

✘ **Do not allow** the victim to smoke.

See overleaf for how to prevent shock from worsening.

Preventing shock from worsening

1 Telephone for an ambulance or ask someone to telephone for you. **2** The victim should lie down. Keep the head low so that gravity can assist the flow of blood to the brain (**a**). The victim should move as little as possible to keep the heart rate down. **3** Stop any bleeding (see pp. 70–3). **4** Reassure the victim. **5** Loosen tight clothing. **6** Use a folded coat or blanket to raise and support the legs (**b**) so that blood will tend to remain in the central area of the body. **7** Cover the victim with a coat or a single blanket (**c**). **8** Check

Shock

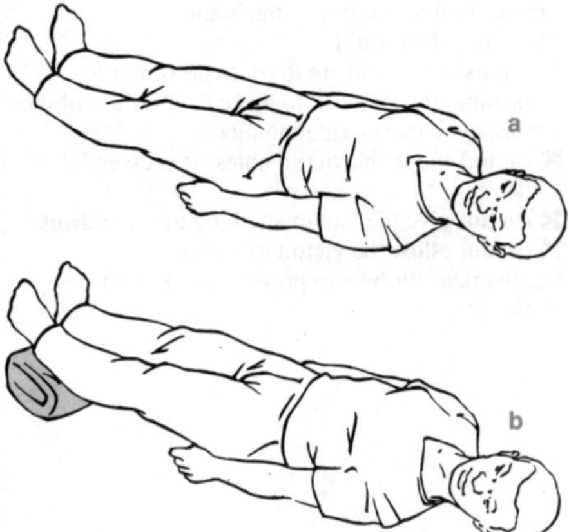

pulse and breathing at frequent intervals – about every couple of minutes.

✖ **Do not use** a hot water bottle to keep the victim warm. This will attract blood to the skin, diverting it from the major organs.

◆ **If the victim** seems likely to vomit, or if breathing becomes difficult or consciousness is lost, place in the recovery position (**d**) (see pp. 31–3).

◆ **If the victim's breathing ceases**, begin artificial ventilation and external chest compression (see pp. 26–8), if necessary.

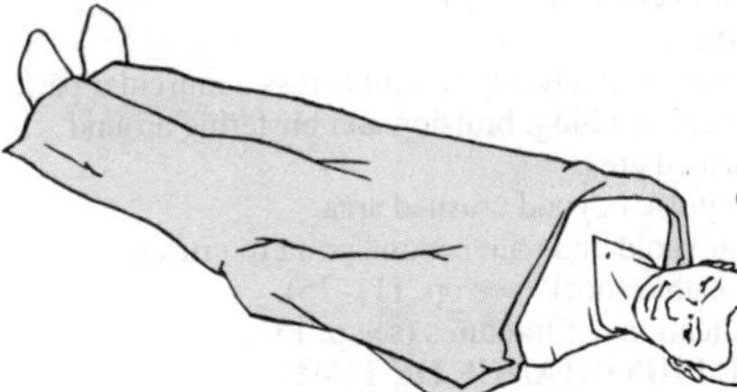

c

d

Crush injuries

These are the kind of injuries sustained when heavy weights fall on the victims. They occur typically when buildings collapse, mines cave in or during the course of serious industrial accidents or earthquakes. In addition to the usual injuries, such as fractures and wounds, crush injuries have special features that affect first aid management. Crushed muscle releases muscle haemoglobin into the blood and this can clog up the kidneys, preventing them from working. Considerable quantities of blood can be lost into crushed muscle.

Features

- Presence of a heavy weight across a muscular part.
- Severe swelling, bruising and blistering around crushed area.
- No pulse beyond crushed area.
- Limb cold and pale beyond point of crushing.
- Probable shock (see pp. 112–15).
- Indications of fractures (see p. 131).

THE IMPORTANCE OF TIME

First aid depends on how long the crushing force has been present.

Less than one hour

1 Remove the crushing weight as quickly as possible (**a**). **2** Get help quickly if you are alone. **3** Call an ambulance. **4** Check the injuries. **5** Check breathing (see pp.17–18) and pulse (**b**) (see p. 21). **6** Control any external bleeding (see pp. 70–3). **7** Treat as for shock (see pp. 114–15). **8** If the victim becomes unconscious place him in the recovery position (see pp. 31–3). **9** Make a note of how long the crushing force persisted and of the time of release. Inform the medical authorities.

✖ **Do not allow the victim to move.**

Crush injuries

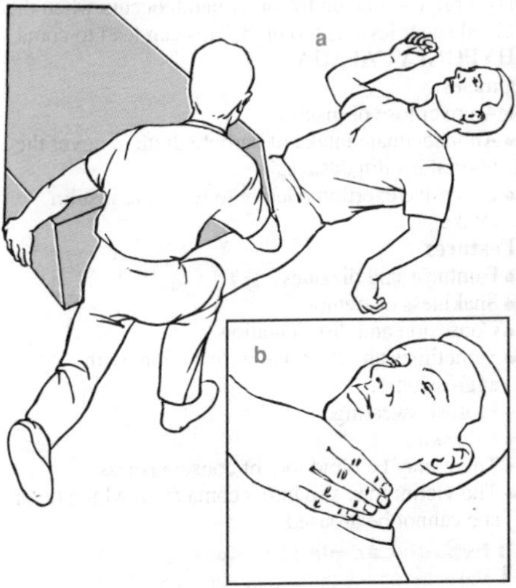

More than one hour

1 Leave the weight in place and explain why to the victim. **2** Call the emergency services and explain the nature of the problem. **3** Reassure the victim.

✖ **After 1 hour, removing the weight** may do more harm than good.

Diabetes

The greatest danger for a diabetic is a severe drop in the level of sugar (glucose) in the blood. This is called hypoglycaemia and it can be very dangerous. Hyperglycaemia, on the other hand, occurs when the blood sugar level is too high. This can lead to coma.

HYPOGLYCAEMIA

Causes

- An overdose of insulin.
- An inadequate intake of carbohydrate to cover the normal insulin dosage.
- Excessive exertion relative to food and insulin intake.

Features

- Faintness and dizziness.
- Shakiness or tremor.
- Confusion and disorientation.
- Sometimes an effect like intoxication, with aggression.
- Profuse sweating.
- Pale skin.
- There may be rapid loss of consciousness.
- The victim may slip into a coma from which he or she cannot be aroused.

If hypoglycaemia is suspected

1 If the person is conscious, give him some sugar, sugary drinks, sweets, chocolate, or other rapidly effective source of carbohydrate, to eat or drink (**a**). This should have a good effect within 10 minutes or so. If so, give more sugar and suggest medical attention. **2** If the victim is unconscious, put him in the recovery position (**b**) (see pp. 31–3). **3** Get the victim to hospital quickly.

Hypoglycaemia

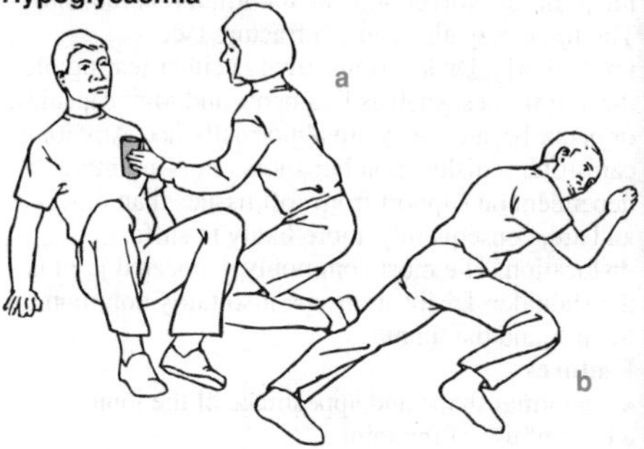

HYPERGLYCAEMIC COMA

Cause

- Too little or no insulin.

Feature

- Victim's breath smells of nail varnish or pear drops.

This is unlikely to be a first aid problem. If it is encountered, the following measures should be taken.

If hyperglycaemia is suspected

1 To ensure that unconsciousness is due to diabetes, look for a diabetic identity disc or card, sugar lumps and needle marks. **2** Put the affected person in the recovery position (see pp. 31–3). **3** Get the victim to hospital quickly.

Dislocations

Dislocations occur at joints when the bones forming the joints are forced into an abnormal relationship. The force may also cause a fracture (see pp. 129–31). Dislocations involve either tearing of the soft tissues, such as ligaments and joint capsules, or occur because they are abnormally lax. Any joint can suffer a dislocation but some joints are more dependent on support from soft tissues than others and are, consequently, more likely to suffer dislocation. The most commonly dislocated joint is the shoulder. Dislocations are also fairly common in the jaw and the thumb.

Features

- Abnormal shape and appearance of the joint.
- Loss of use of the joint.
- Swelling and bruising around the joint.
- Usually severe pain, unless the dislocation has occurred many times before.

DISLOCATED SHOULDER

The head of the upper arm bone (humerus) sits in a very shallow hollow in the side of the shoulder blade (**a**) and is easily displaced downwards and inwards (**b**). Dislocation usually results from a fall on the outstretched hand. The capsule of the joint tears and the head of the bone slips though the gap.

Features

- The arm appears too long and the profile of the shoulder appears abnormal with a sharp angle (**b**).
- The casualty may prefer to support the arm on the dislocated side with the other hand.

✘ **Do not attempt to move** or 'click' the bones back into position. This could damage the surrounding nerves and tissue or, if one is present, make the fracture worse.

In the event of dislocation

1 Support the injured shoulder in the most comfortable position. **2** Maintain it in this position with a pillow or cushion (**c**), sling or bandages (see pp. 243–6). **3** Arrange for transport to hospital.

✘ **Avoid giving food or drink**, as a general anaesthetic may be needed.

Dislocated shoulder

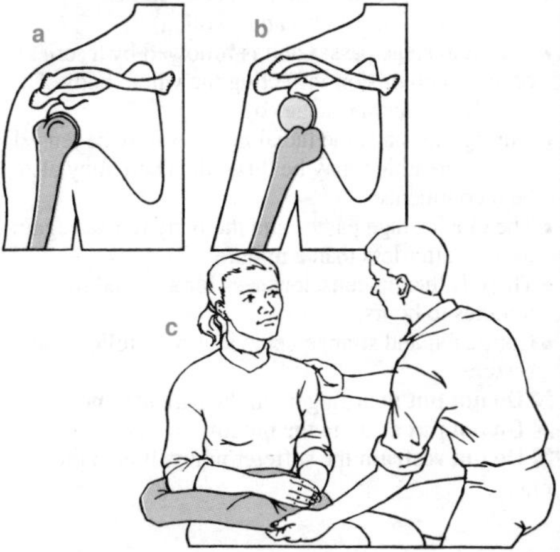

Epilepsy

This takes various forms but first aid is likely to be required only for major epilepsy (*grand mal*). This is the type most people think of as epilepsy. A *grand mal* attack usually comes on suddenly but some epileptics experience a warning of an impending attack in the form of odd body sensations (the aura).

Features

- The person suddenly loses consciousness and falls.
- This may be accompanied by a cry.
- The body becomes stiff. This is called the tonic stage (**a**).
- The breathing stops and the face becomes congested (purplish-red and swollen).
- The rigid stage passes and is followed by a series of jerky convulsions affecting the whole body. This is called the clonic stage (**b**).
- During this stage the facial muscles may be tensed up and breathing may be difficult. There may also be incontinence.
- The clonic stage passes and the body relaxes again, usually after less than a minute.
- There is then unconsciousness for a period of minutes to hours.
- Confusion and strange behaviour may follow the seizure.

✘ **Do not put** your fingers in the patient's mouth.

✘ **Do not put** a gag in the mouth.

✘ **Do not restrain** the sufferer unless it is to prevent injury.

Stages of epilepsy

a

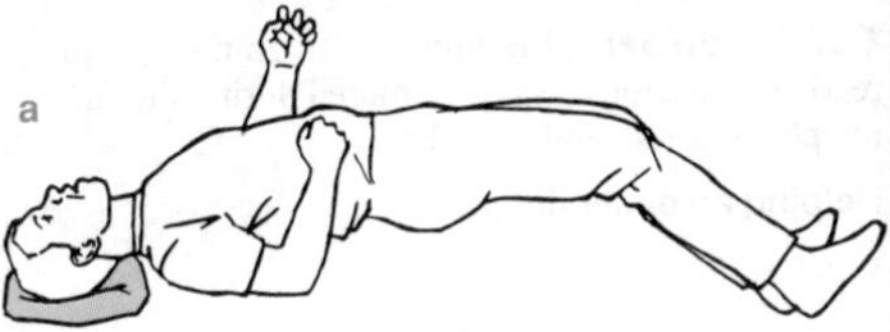

b

Helping an epileptic

1 At the onset, try to help the victim to fall safely (**a**; see overleaf). **2** Put some form of padding, such as a rolled-up coat, under the head. **3** Clear a space around the victim, to minimize possible injury. **4** Check pockets for an epilepsy card. This may give information on what pattern the seizures normally take. **5** Stay with the victim until you are sure the attack is over. **6** If the convulsions continue for more than a minute or two, send for an ambulance. Otherwise, do not. **7** Put the victim into the recovery position (**b**) (see pp. 31–3) once the convulsions have stopped.

◆ **If the sufferer takes longer** than 15 minutes to recover consciousness or is injured during the fit, telephone for an ambulance.

Helping an epileptic

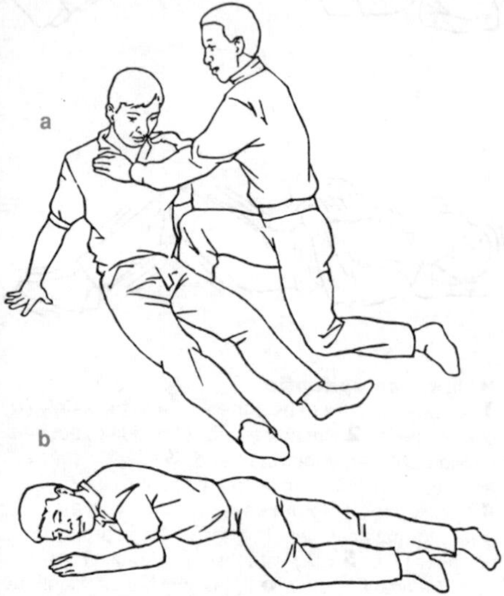

Extremes of body temperature

The body has excellent temperature regulating mechanisms and can normally be relied on to keep internal temperature within narrow limits. If, however, the body is exposed to high or low temperatures for long periods, the heat regulation process may not be adequate to maintain normal body temperature. This may result in abnormally high or abnormally low internal body temperature: respectively, heatstroke and hypothermia.

HEATSTROKE

This dangerous condition is due to the breakdown of the body's heat-regulating mechanisms, as a result of exposure to very high temperatures. The body temperature rises from the normal 37 °C (98.6 °F) to 41 °C (105.8 °F) or higher. Emergency measures are necessary to get the temperature down quickly if life is to be saved.

Features

- The victim may become unconscious.
- The victim is restless and dizzy.
- The victim complains of feeling hot and having a headache.
- The skin is hot and dry.
- The pulse is strong and fast.
- The victim may become confused.
- Coma may result.

Management of heatstroke

1 Summon medical help and explain what is happening. **2** Place the victim in a half-lying, half-sitting position (**a**; see overleaf). **3** Remove all the

victim's clothing. **4** Wrap him in a cold wet sheet. **5** Keep the sheet wet with cold water (**b**).
6 Fan the sheet so that evaporation cools the victim more effectively (**c**). **7** Stop when the skin feels cool or the temperature falls to 38 °C (100.4 °F).
8 Watch out for a second rise in body temperature. Repeat steps 4 to 6, if necessary.

♦ **If the victim is unconscious**, cool him in the recovery position (see pp. 31–3). Check breathing and pulse (see pp. 17–18 and 21).

Management of heatstroke

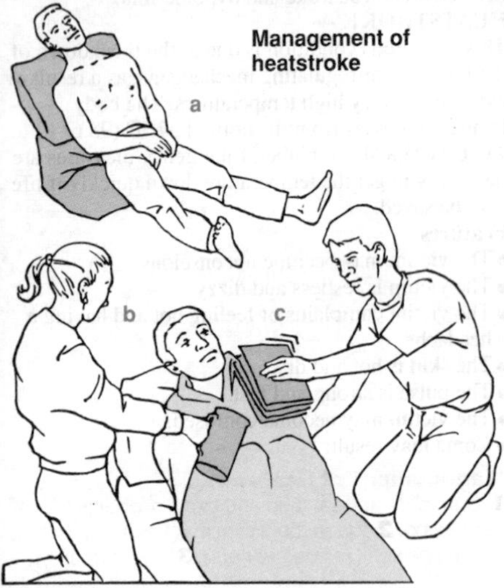

HYPOTHERMIA

This condition arises where the body's temperature drops below the normal level of 37 °C (98.6 °F). If, for example, heat is constantly carried away by cold winds, the body's heat-production process (shivering) may cease to function adequately. Elderly and frail people, especially if thin, tired and hungry, are most liable to hypothermia, particularly in inadequately heated or unheated houses.

Features

- There is early shivering, which may pass off.
- The skin is cold and dry.
- The pulse is slow.
- The victim's rate of breathing is slow.
- The measured body temperature is 35 °C (95 °F) or less.
- There is drowsiness which may progress to coma.
- There may be cardiac arrest (see pp. 108–9).

Aims of first aid

The aim is to warm the body gradually but with minimum delay. Never assume that a hypothermic victim has died unless this is obvious. Hypothermia protects the brain against lack of oxygen and a person can survive a longer than usual period of cardiac arrest.

Management of hypothermia: outdoors

1 Send for medical help. **2** Get the victim into a sheltered place or indoors as soon as possible. **3** Use a sleeping bag, or other form of insulation, to cover the victim (**a**; see overleaf). **4** Share your own body heat with the victim under a common cover. **5** Check for breathing (see pp. 17–18). ►►

6 Check for pulse (see p. 21). **7** Give hot drinks and food, if available.

Management of hypothermia: indoors
1 Send for medical help. **2** If the victim is conscious and uninjured, put him in a warmed bed. Make sure the head (but not the face) is covered, too. **3** Give hot drinks and food (**b**).

Management of hypothermia

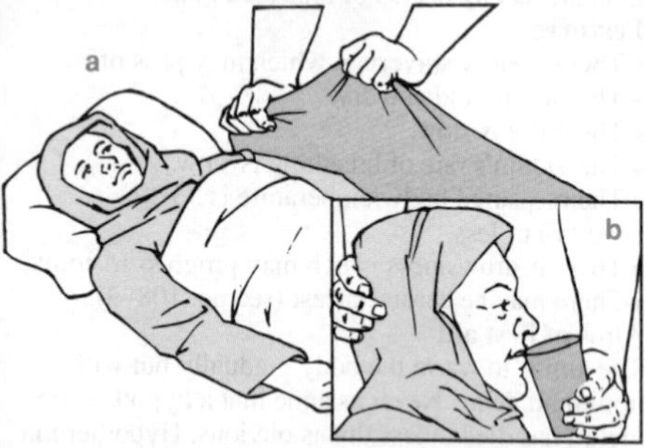

♦ **If the victim is unconscious**, resuscitate, if necessary, by mouth-to-mouth ventilation and chest compression.
✖ **Do not rub** the victim's limbs or encourage vigorous movement.
✖ **Do not allow** the victim to drink any alcohol. This causes heat loss.
✖ **Do not immerse** the victim in a hot bath or use hot water bottles. This will divert blood from the major organs to the superficial vessels of the skin.

Fractures

A fracture is a break or a crack in a bone. Generally, before fractures are dealt with, the first aider should pay attention to any breathing difficulty (see pp. 17–20 and 74), severe bleeding (see pp. 70–3 and 34–5) and unconsciousness (see pp. 173–5).

TYPES OF FRACTURE

Closed (a)

The skin is intact and the bone, however badly damaged, remains uninfected. Swelling and bruising may not be evident immediately.

Open (b)

A broken bone end protrudes through the skin, or there is a skin wound that is connected with the fracture site. Open fractures must always be assumed to be infected.

Complicated (c)

These arise where the fractured ends or fragments of bone have caused injury to important adjacent parts such as arteries, nerves or organs.

Types of fracture

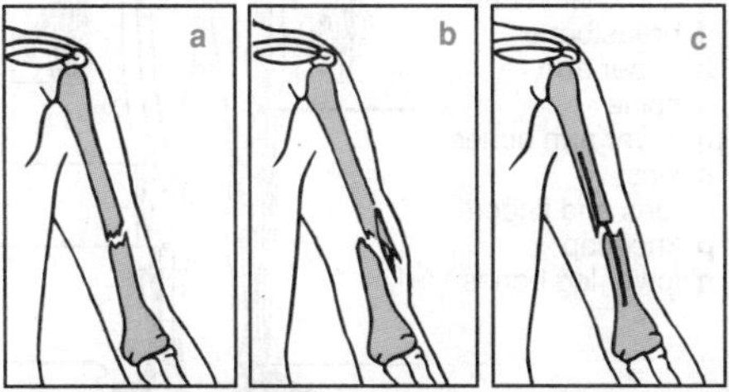

CAUSES AND SITES OF FRACTURE

Any bone in the body can be fractured by direct violence, by bending or twisting, by force transmitted along a bone, by excessive stress from the muscle pull or by disease that weakens bone. Old bones break more easily and more cleanly than young bones, which often suffer incomplete (greenstick) fractures.

Some fractures are more common than others. The sites of the most common fractures are shown below.

Sites of fracture

- **a** skull
- **b** collarbone
- **c** ribs
- **d** elbow
- **e** pelvis
- **f** neck of the thigh bone
- **g** shaft of thigh bone
- **h** ankle
- **i** nose, jaw and cheekbone
- **j** breastbone
- **k** upper arm
- **l** spine
- **m** lower arm bones
- **n** wrist
- **o** toes and fingers
- **p** kneecap
- **q** lower leg bones

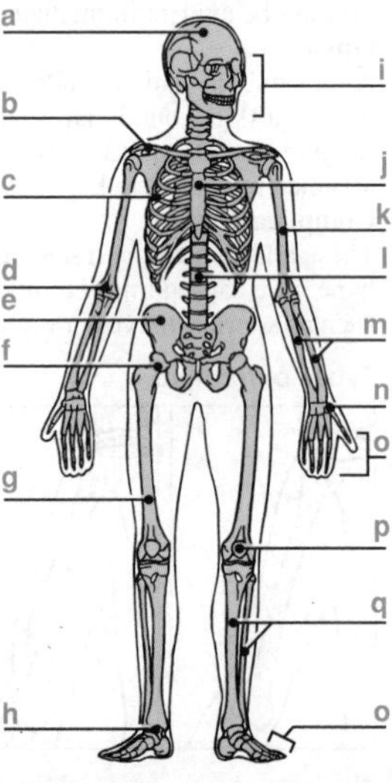

SYMPTOMS AND SIGNS OF FRACTURE

- Pain and tenderness to touch (**a**).
- Swelling, bruising (**b**) and deformity (**c**), such as irregularity in the line of the bone or shortening of the affected limb.
- Abnormal movement or instability.
- The injured limb does not function as well as it did, if at all.
- A grating sensation on attempts at movement (crepitus)
- There may be features of shock (see p. 113).

✖ **Do not move** a victim with a fracture unless it is absolutely essential.

✖ **No attempt** should ever be made to test for crepitus. This may cause further injury.

Symptoms and signs of fracture

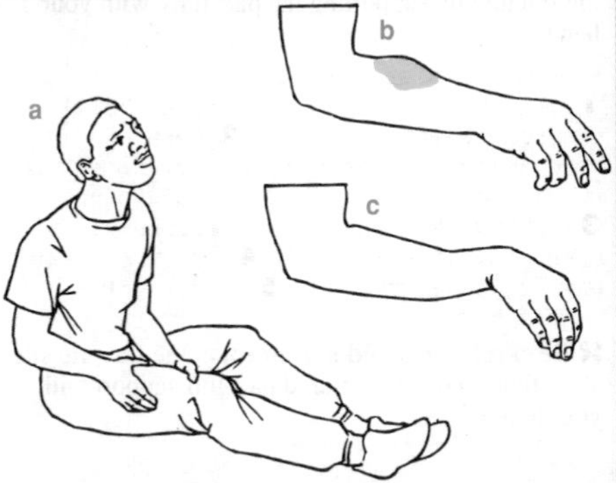

OPEN FRACTURES

Features

- There is always a wound near the fracture site.
- Protruding bone ends might be visible.

Where the bone is not protruding

1 Telephone for an ambulance. **2** If there is much bleeding, apply pressure if possible (**a**). **3** Squeeze the edges of the wound together, to control bleeding (see pp. 70–3). **4** Cover with a pad of clean material such as a folded handkerchief (**b**). Use sterile gauze, if available. **5** Secure the covering with a pad and a firm bandage (**c**) (see pp. 226–8). **6** Immobilize the injured part (see pp. 134–9 and 243–5) and get the victim to hospital.

✘ **Do not tie** the bandage too tight as this might impair circulation.

✘ **While performing this procedure**, avoid moving the fracture by supporting the part fully with your hand.

Where the bone protrudes

1 Place sterile gauze, if available, or a piece of clean cloth over the wound (**a**). **2** Place a ring of cotton wool around the open wound, over the gauze (**b**). It must be higher than the protruding bone. **3** Fix this in place with a secure, diagonally-placed bandage (**c**) (see pp. 236–7). **4** Immobilize the part (see pp. 134–9 and 243–5). **5** Arrange for the victim's transport to hospital.

✘ **Be careful to avoid** movement at the fracture site at all times. Give the injured part full support with your hands.

Where the bone is not protruding

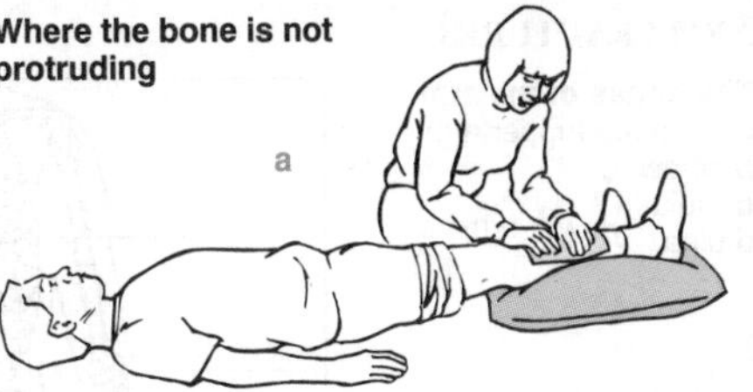

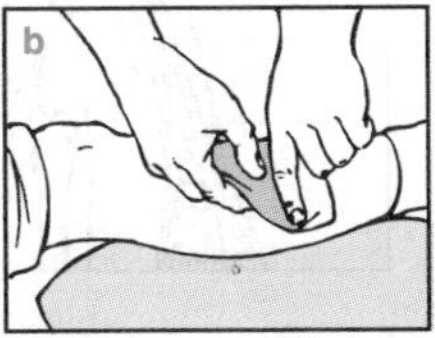

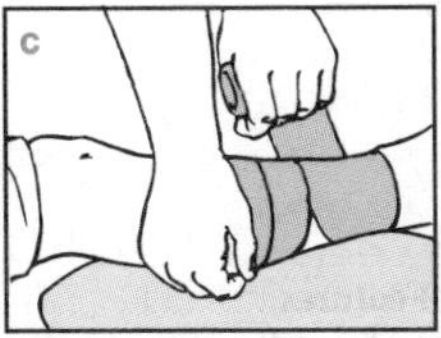

Where the bone protrudes

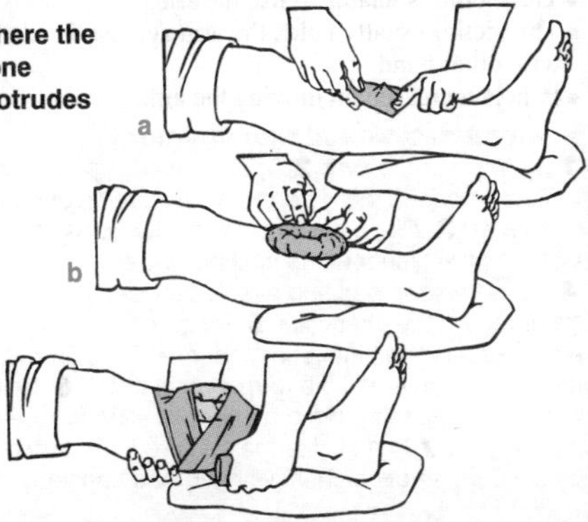

ARM FRACTURES

The bones of the arm

a humerus (upper arm)
b elbow
c radius } lower arm
d ulna

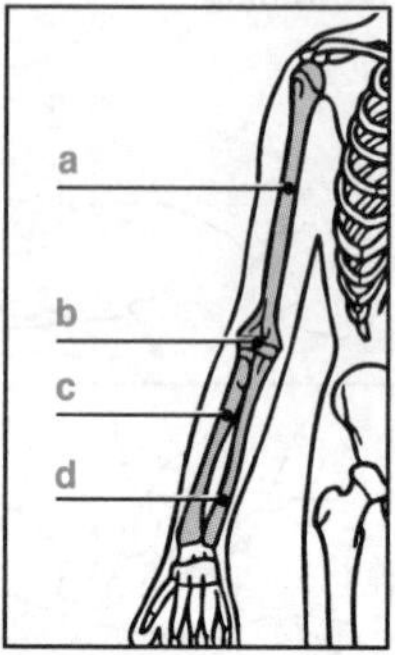

Features

- The victim is unable to use the arm.
- The victim usually holds the arm against the chest with other hand.
- Pain is increased on moving the arm.

Immobilization and management

1 Sit the victim down. **2** Check the wrist pulse (see p. 21). If absent, the urgency for hospital treatment is greater. **3** Place the forearm gently across the victim's chest, supporting it all the while.
4 Put some soft padding evenly between the fracture and the chest (**a**). **5** For extra support, place a rolled-up blanket or coat on the victim's lap, allowing the injured limb to rest upon it (**b**). **6** While carefully supporting the arm, apply a sling (**c**) (see pp. 243–4). **7** Immobilize the fractured arm further by securing it to the chest with a broad bandage

(see p. 238), applied over the sling (**d**). **8** Transport the patient to hospital in a sitting position.

✖ **Avoid undue pressure** on the fracture.

Forearm fractures. These need not be padded.

Immobilizing the arm

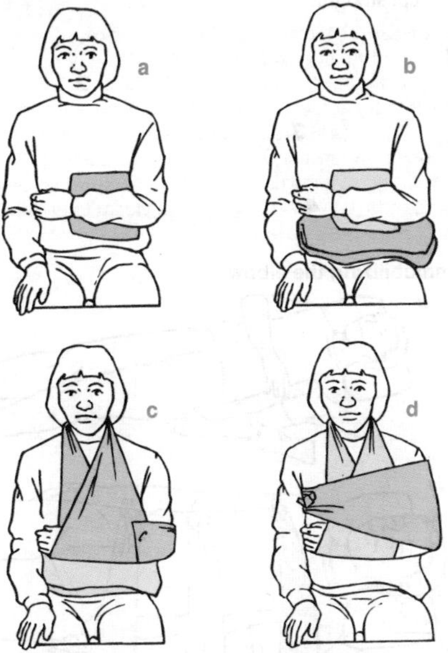

ELBOW FRACTURES

Features

- The victim is unable to bend the elbow.
- There is severe pain on attempts to bend the elbow.
- The pulse may be absent at the wrist.

✘ **Do not attempt** to bend the elbow. The arm must be kept straight.

Immobilization and management

1 The victim should lie down, the first aider supporting the arm on the injured side. **2** Place some soft padding between the victim's side and the injured arm (**a**). **3** Strap the injured arm to the body, at the upper arm and chest, at the forearm and waist, and at the wrist and hips, using three broad bandages (**b**). **4** Arrange for the victim to be taken to hospital lying down.

Immobilizing the elbow

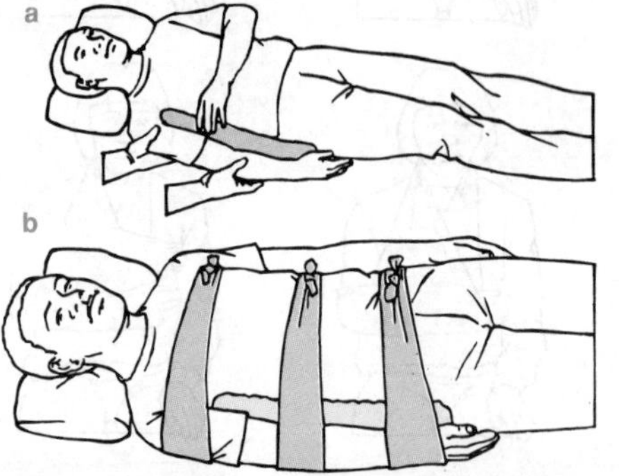

COLLARBONE FRACTURES

The collarbones

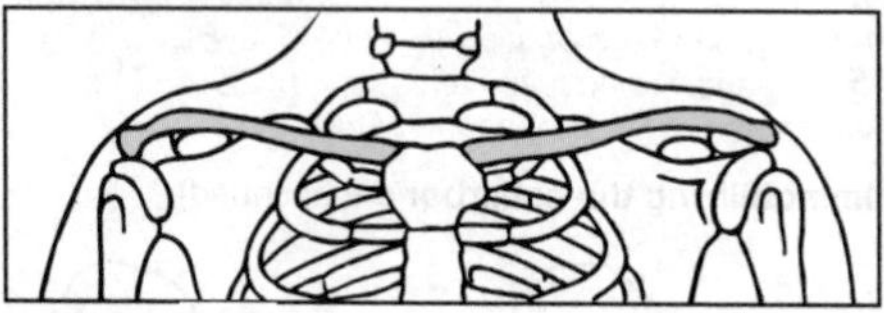

Features

- Swelling and deformity at the site.
- Pain on moving the arm on the side of the fracture.
- The arm on the injured side loses some ability to move.
- The victim will tend to support the arm on the injured side.

Immobilization and management

1 Sit the victim down. **2** Put some loose padding in the armpit on the side of the fracture (**a**). ►►

Immobilizing the collarbone

3 Put the arm in a sling (see pp. 243–5) and carefully pull the sling high, so that the fingertips are at shoulder level (**b**). **4** Fix the arm to the body with a broad bandage or sling (**c**) (see p. 238).
5 Transport to hospital in a sitting position. The victim may walk to hospital if able.

Immobilizing the collarbone (continued)

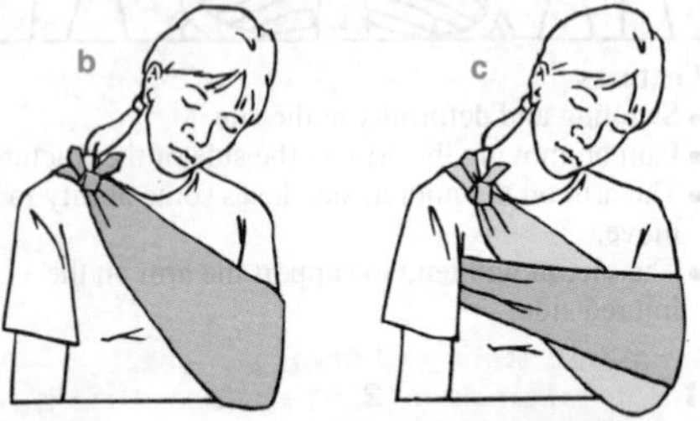

WRIST, HAND AND FINGER FRACTURES

The wrist, hand and finger bones
a wrist bones
b hand bones
c finger bones

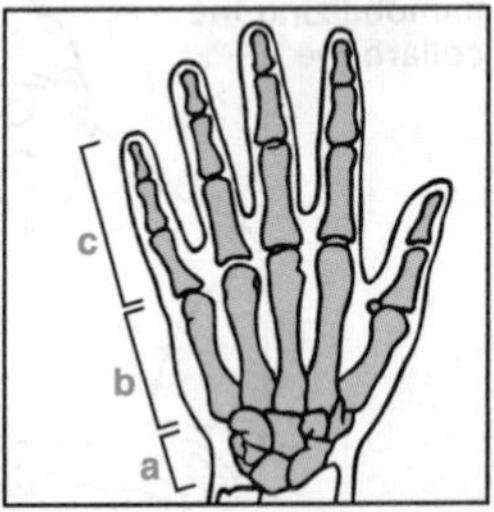

Features

- Bleeding or marked discolouration and swelling.
- The victim is unable to make a fist.

Immobilization and management

1 Control any bleeding. **2** Check the wrist pulse (**a**) (see p. 21), without moving the hand, to ensure blood supply is not restricted by injury. **3** Pad the hand and wrist with soft material for protection (**b**). **4** Apply an elevation sling (see pp. 244–6). **5** Gently pull the sling high so that the hand is well above the level of the elbow (**c**). **6** Fix the upper arm to the body with a broad bandage or sling (**d**) (see p. 238). **7** Transport to hospital in a sitting position.

Immobilizing the hand and wrist

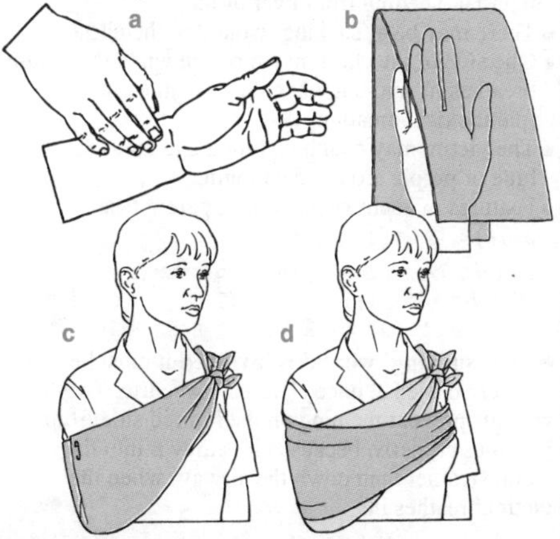

RIB AND BREASTBONE FRACTURES

The ribs and breastbone
a ribcage
b breastbone

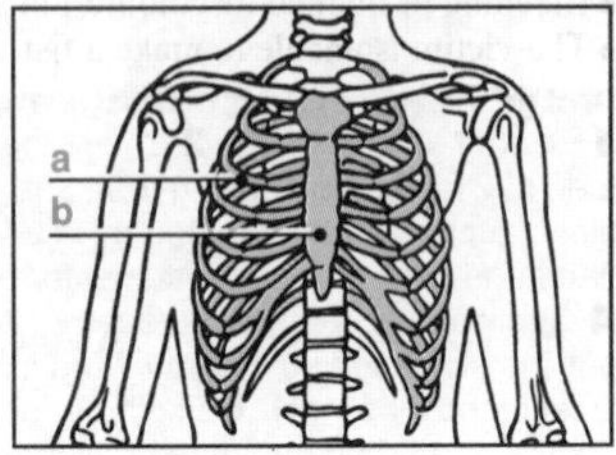

Features

- Sharp pain on breathing in.
- Possible restlessness or shock (see p. 113) from internal bleeding from liver or lung.
- There may be a 'sucking' wound in the chest.
- One side of the chest may move in when the victim breathes in, and out when they breathe out (paradoxical breathing).
- The victim may cough up blood and may be blue or purple around the mouth.
- Features of asphyxia may be apparent (see p. 74).

Immobilization and management

1 Put the arm on the injured side in an elevation sling (see pp. 244–6). **2** Get the victim to hospital.

♦ **If a 'sucking' wound is involved** it must be securely closed at once. This can save life. These wounds prevent the lung on the injured side from inflating properly, because air is drawn into the wound (rather than down the airway) when the victim breathes in.

Treating a 'sucking' wound

1 If possible, encourage the patient to cough. **2** Use your hand to form an airtight seal (**a**). **3** To make a more effective and permanent seal, place a sterile dressing or clean handkerchief over the wound (**b**). **4** Cover the dressing with a sheet of plastic or foil (**c**), tape the covering to the chest and ensure that breathing is normal. **5** Put the arm on the injured side in an elevation sling (**d**) (see pp. 244–6). **6** Place the victim in a half-sitting, half-lying position, inclined to the injured side (**e**). **7** Use the recovery position (see pp. 31–3), if consciousness is lost. **8** Get the victim to hospital quickly.

Treating a 'sucking' wound

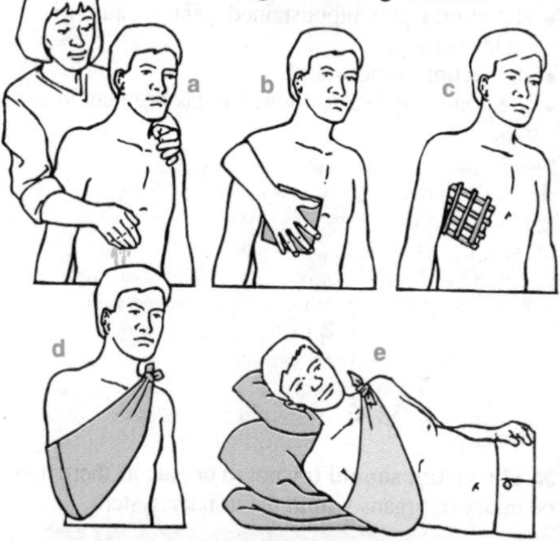

PELVIS FRACTURES

The pelvis and bones of the hip and thigh
a pelvis
b hip (neck of thigh bone)
c shaft of thigh bone

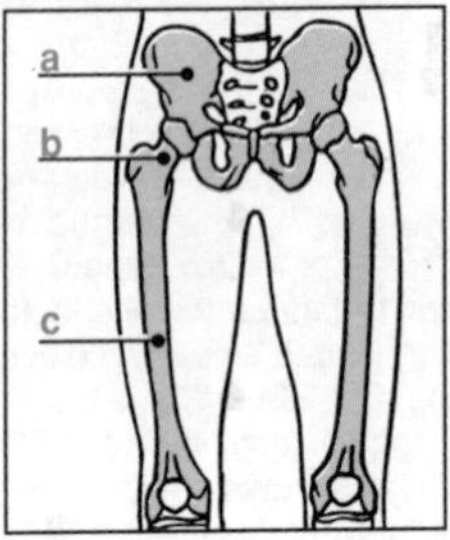

Features

- Severe pain in the hips, lower back or groin.
- Signs of shock (see p. 113).
- Victim may pass bloodstained urine because of bladder injury.
- The victim cannot stand.
- The body may feel as though it has been cut in two.

Immobilization and management

1 The victim should be left on his back (with some kind of support beneath the bent knees, if this is more comfortable) (**a**). **2** Wrap two broad bandages or slings around the pelvis (**b**) and tie them tightly, with knots on the unaffected side, unless this causes severe pain. **3** Put padding between the legs (**c**). **4** Tie the legs together at the knees and ankles (**d**). **5** If necessary, treat the victim for shock (see pp. 114–15). **6** Transport the victim to hospital lying down.

✖ **The victim should try** not to urinate as there may be injury to organs within the urinary system.

Immobilizing the pelvis

a

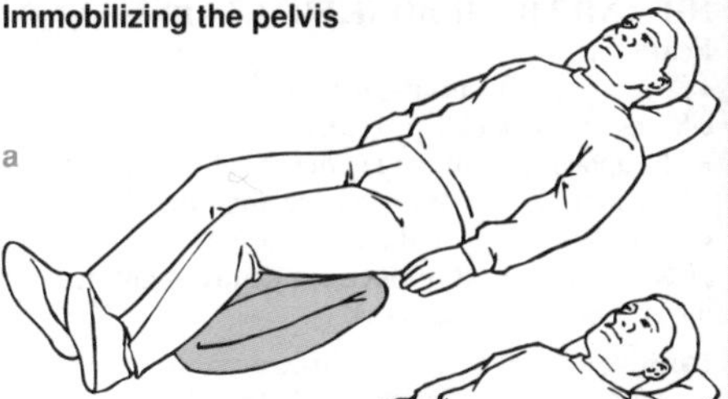

b

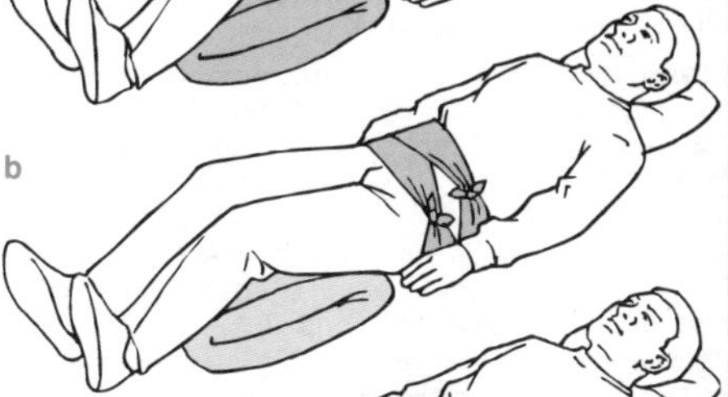

c

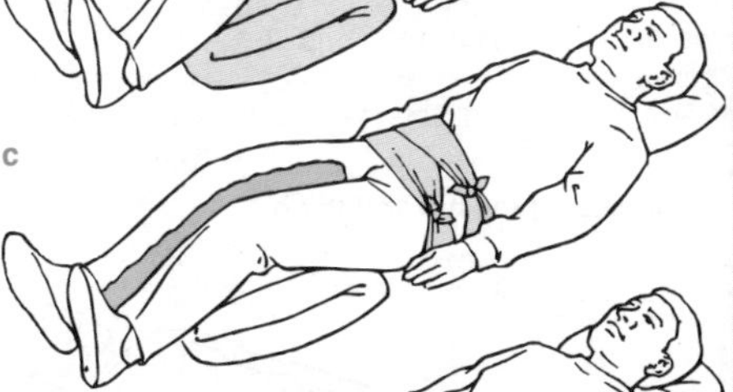

d

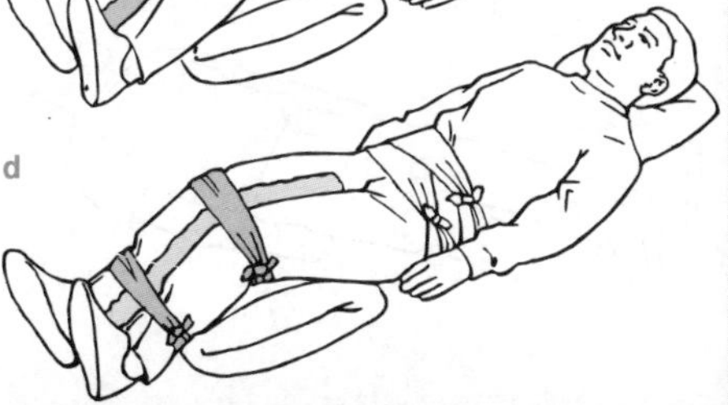

HIP AND THIGH-BONE FRACTURES

Features

- Severe bruising around the hip.
- Signs of shock (see p. 113).
- The appearance of the leg may be deformed: it may look shorter or be twisted abnormally.
- Possible swelling at the fracture site.

✖ **Remember that unnecessary movement** may dangerously increase shock.

Immobilization and management

1 Telephone for an ambulance immediately.
2 Gently but firmly pull on the foot to straighten the leg, while giving full support around the fracture with your hands. **3** Align the two legs by moving the healthy leg towards the injured one. **4** Check whether the fracture is closed or open, and treat accordingly (see pp. 132–3). **5** Put padding between the legs (**a**). **6** Bandage them together (**b**). Use a figure-of-eight bandage at the ankles and feet (see p. 241). **7** Treat for shock, if necessary.

Immobilizing the hip and thigh

a

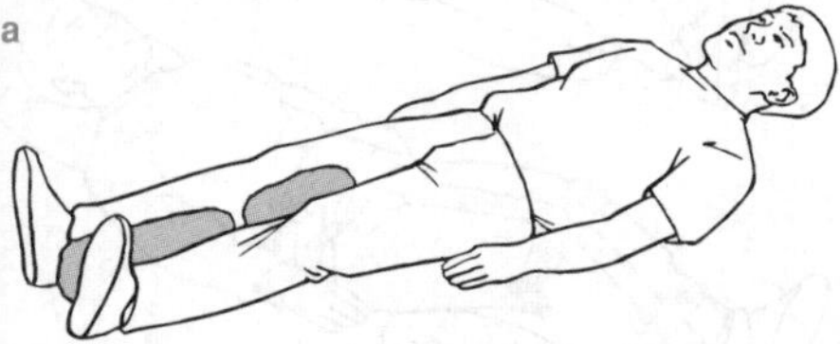

Immobilizing the hip and thigh (continued)

b

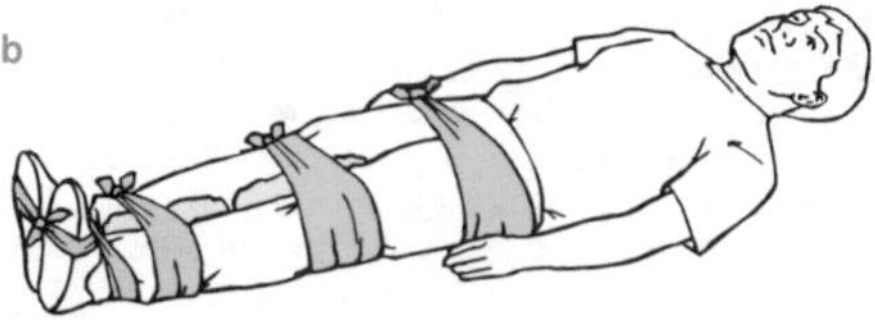

8 Reassure the patient. **9** Loosen tight clothing. **10** Cover the victim with a coat, if very cold, but do not overheat. **11** Get the victim to hospital quickly.

✖ **Do not bandage** over the fracture site.

LOWER LEG FRACTURES

The bones of the lower leg
a kneecap
b tibia (shin bone)
c fibula

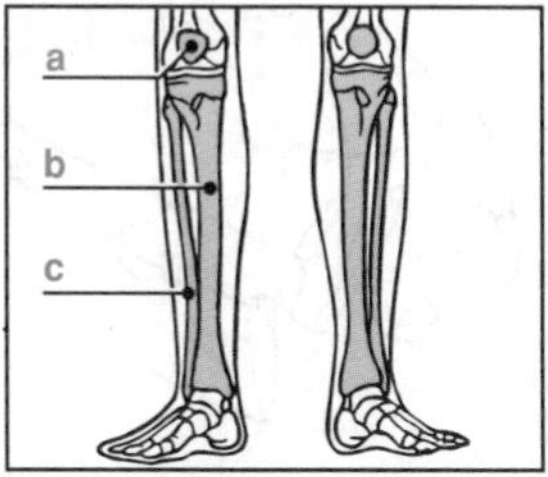

Features

- Abnormal angle of foot and leg is usually apparent.
- Irregularity in the line of the bone can often be felt.
- There is obvious swelling and bruising.
- The bone is often visible in open fractures.
- The patient may be suffering from shock.

Immobilization and management

1 The victim should lie down. **2** Support the leg by holding it above and below the fracture site (**a**). **3** Check whether the fracture is closed or open, and treat accordingly (see pp. 132–3). **4** Put padding between the ankles and legs, and bind both legs together with broad bandages or slings (**b**). **6** It may be necessary to treat the victim for shock (see pp. 114–15). **7** Get the victim to hospital.

✘ **Do not bandage** over the fracture site.

Immobilizing the lower leg

a

Immobilizing the lower leg (continued)

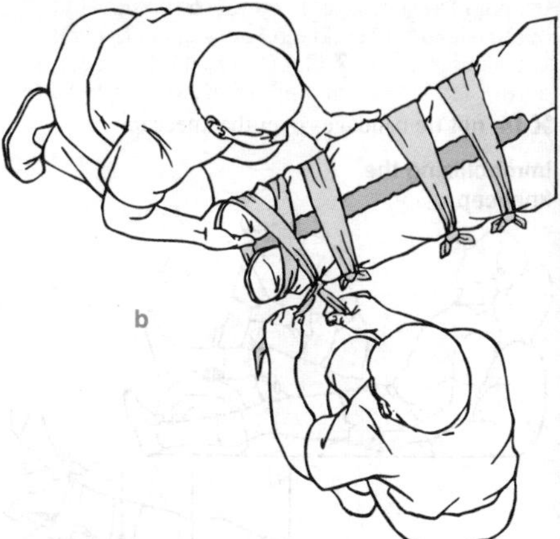

KNEECAP FRACTURES

Features

- Tenderness over the kneecap.
- Severe swelling of the knee.
- Pain on attempts to straighten the knee.

Immobilization and management

1 Place the victim in a half-lying, half-sitting position, with the head and shoulders supported. **2** Gently straighten the affected leg. **3** Raise it to a comfortable position (**a**; see overleaf). **4** Put a padded board (**b**; see overleaf) under the leg that extends from buttock to heel. ►►

5 Put extra padding under the natural hollows beneath the knee and ankle (**c**). **6** Tie the leg to the board with broad bandages or slings at the ankle, thigh and shin (**d**). **7** Get the victim to hospital, lying down, with the foot of the injured leg raised.

✖ **Do not tie** bandages over the kneecap.

Immobilizing the kneecap

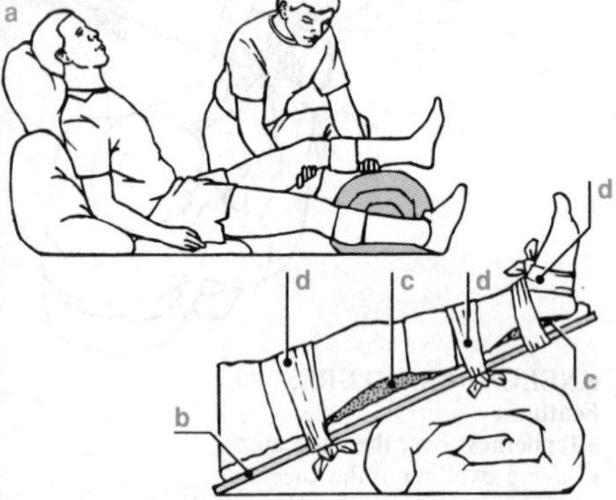

FOOT FRACTURES

The bones of the foot
a toe bones
b instep bones
c heel bone

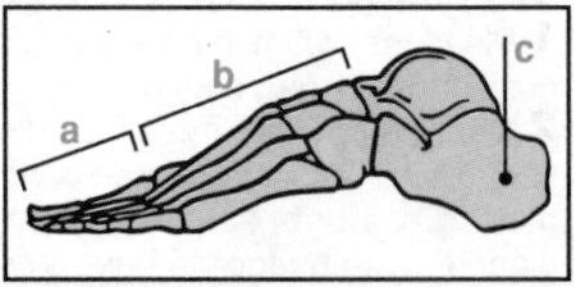

Features

- Inability to take weight on the foot.
- Deformity of the arch of the foot.
- Severe swelling and bruising.

Immobilization and management

1 The victim should lie down. **2** Very gently ease off the shoe and sock (**a**). Cut laces, if necessary. **3** Raise and support the foot with a large pad behind the ankle (**b**). **4** Cover any open fracture (see pp. 132–3). **5** Control any bleeding with a pad and bandage (**c**). **6** Transport to hospital with the foot raised. **7** A padded board (**d**) under the foot may aid comfort. It should be fixed using a figure-of-eight bandage (see p. 239).

Immobilizing the foot

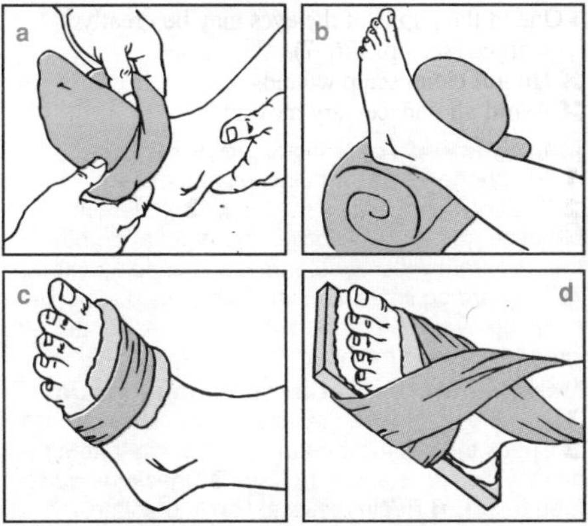

SKULL FRACTURES

Sites of fracture

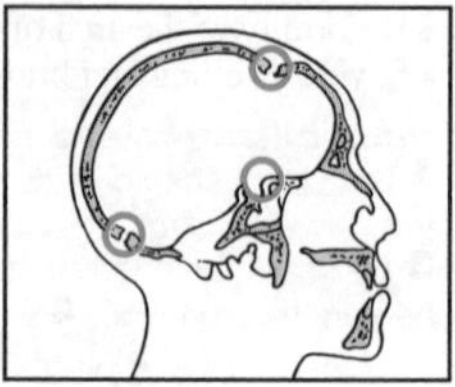

Features

- The victim may lose consciousness.
- There may be a boggy depression in the scalp.
- There may be bleeding from the ear.
- There may be watery fluid dripping from nose or ears.
- One of the pupils of the eyes may be greatly enlarged (see pp. 176–7).

✘ **Do not clean** scalp wounds.

✘ **Avoid** all unnecessary movement.

Management for a conscious victim

1 Telephone for an ambulance immediately.
2 Position the victim on the back. **3** If there is bleeding from the ear, incline the head and body to the side from which fluid or blood is dripping (**a**).
4 To guard against infection, lightly place a sterile dressing over the ear. Secure it with a bandage wrapped around the head (**b**).

Management for an unconscious victim

1 Telephone for an ambulance immediately.
2 Check the victim's breathing, ensuring that the airway is clear (see pp. 18–20). **3** Check the pulse (see p. 21). **4** Begin resuscitation immediately, if

breathing and heartbeat stop (see pp. 22–9). **5** Place the victim in the recovery position (see pp. 31–3). **6** If there is bleeding from the ear, place the victim so that the affected ear is lower. **7** Cover the ear with a sterile dressing.

Management: conscious victim

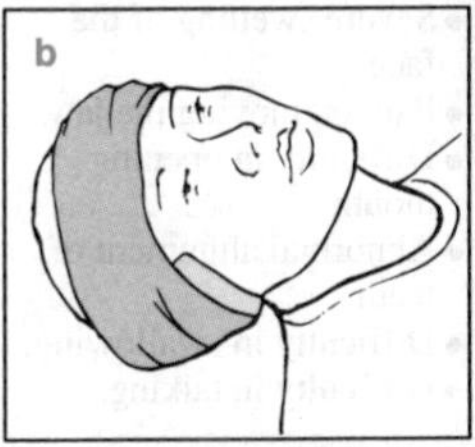

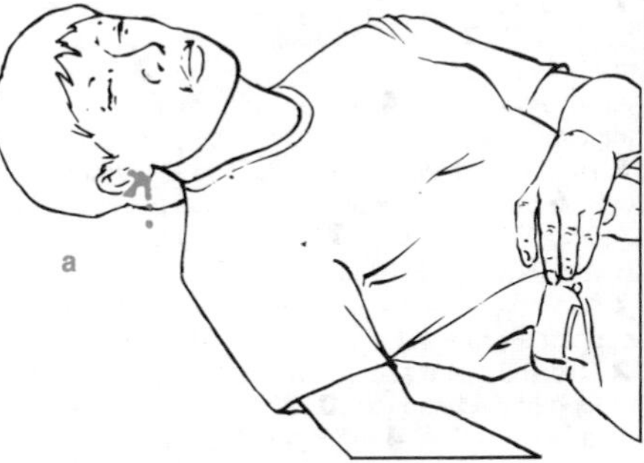

NOSE, CHEEKBONE AND JAW FRACTURES

Sites of fracture
a nose
b cheekbone
c jaw

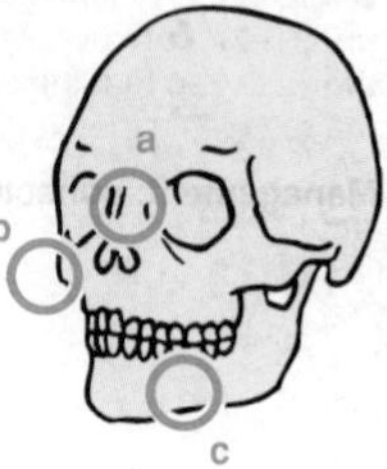

Features

- Severe swelling of the face.
- Pain on moving the jaw.
- Difficulty in opening mouth.
- Abnormal alignment of teeth.
- Difficulty in swallowing.
- Difficulty in talking.

Management

1 Ensure that the airway is clear and open (see pp. 18–20). **2** Incline the victim forward to allow any fluid in the mouth and nose to run out. **3** Telephone for an ambulance. **4** Use a cold compress over the affected area to reduce swelling, bleeding and pain. **5** Treat the nosebleed (see pp. 196–8), if there is one. **6** See to the mouth wound (see pp. 70–3, 202–3), if there is one. **7** Get the victim to hospital.

If the jaw is dislocated

1 As long as breathing is not adversely affected, support the jaw with a pad under the chin (**a**).
2 This should be secured with a bandage tied on the top of the head (**b**). **3** Put the victim in the recovery position. **4** Place a soft piece of padding under the victim's head to keep the weight off the injured jaw (**c**). **5** Get the victim to hospital.

Immobilizing the jaw

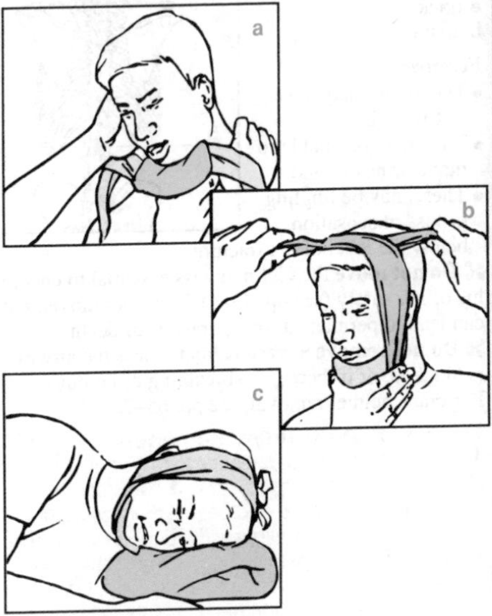

✖ **The bandage must** not be so tight that the jaws are locked together.

◆ **If the victim vomits**, untie the bandage and support the head and jaw. Clean the mouth gently before replacing the pad and bandage.

NECK FRACTURES

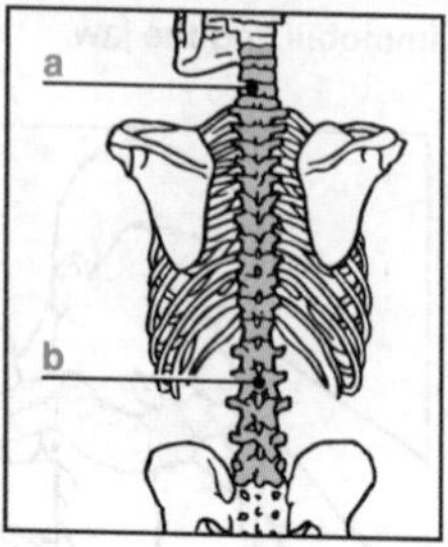

The neck and spine
a neck
b spine

Features

- The victim may have a stiff neck.
- They may be unable to move arms or legs.
- There may be tingling or loss of sensation below the level of the fracture.

✘ **Do not move** the victim unless essential to ensure his or her safety (see pp. 43–4). Improper movement can lead to permanent total paralysis or death.

✘ **Do not remove** a crash helmet unless the airway is blocked, or if there is no breathing or no pulse. For crash helmet removal, see pp. 65–7.

Immobilization and management

1 Telephone for an ambulance immediately.
2 Leave victim flat on the back. **3** Reassure the victim. **4** Squat above and behind the victim's head and keep the head straight with your hands over the ears (**a**). **5** A firm (cervical) collar round the neck, made from rolled-up newspaper can help, but you must continue to hold the head straight.

Making and applying a cervical collar

Two first aiders will be required. **1** Roll a newspaper in cloth (**b**). **2** Place the centre of the collar under the chin and wrap it around the neck (**c**). **3** Secure it with a scarf knotted at the front (**d**). **4** Check the breathing.

Immobilizing the neck

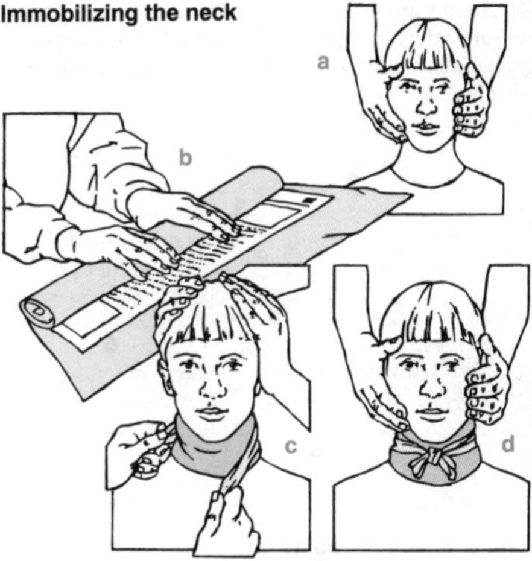

✘ **The head should be held** absolutely still during and after the application of the collar.

✘ **Do not wrap** the collar around the neck too tightly.

♦ **If there is no suitable paper available**, the head should be held until professional help arrives.

SPINE FRACTURES

Features

- There may be severe back pain.
- There may be loss of use of legs and arms.
- There may be tingling or loss of sensation below the fracture.

✖ **Do not move** the victim unless it is essential to ensure safety (see pp. 43–4 and 58–60). Improper movement can lead to permanent total paralysis or death.

Immobilization and management

Two first aiders will be required. **1** Tell the victim to try not to move. **2** Check breathing (see pp. 17–18) and circulation (see p. 21). **3** Telephone for an ambulance immediately. **4** One person should squat above and behind the victim's head, holding it with the hands over the victim's ears (**a**). The head should be kept straight. **5** Support the victim's trunk with rolled-up clothes on either side (**b**). **6** Put soft padding between the legs and bind them together at hips, thighs and ankles (**c**). **7** If vomiting is imminent, turn the victim into the spinal recovery position (opposite). **8** Make sure that the airway remains clear. **9** Transport the victim to hospital, lying down.

Immobilizing the spine

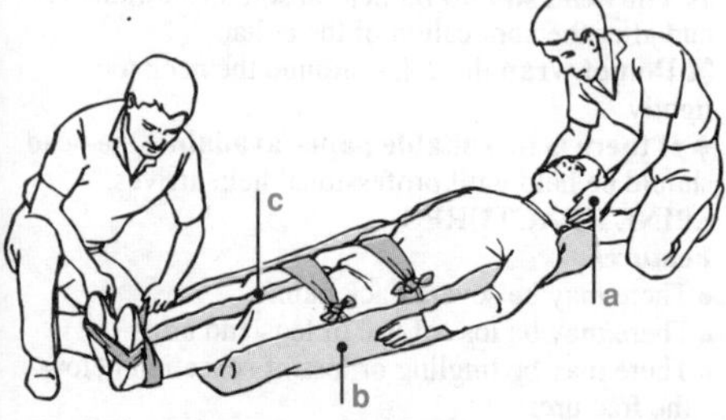

Spinal recovery position

This must be adopted only if the victim is unconscious. **1** Six people are required. One ensures that the head, neck and body always remain in line, to avoid further injury. This person gives orders to the others. **2** Three people kneel on one side, two on the other. **3** Turn the victim on to his or her front, if necessary. **4** The three helpers must carefully roll the victim on to the side with the raised arm, avoiding twisting the spine, while the two on the other side carefully lift (**b**; see overleaf). **5** Move the victim's lower arm under the head to help keep the neck straight (**c**; see overleaf), and bend the upper leg so that the knee is on the ground and the foot on the calf of the other leg (**d**; see overleaf). Continue to keep the head, neck and body in alignment. **6** Apply a neck collar (see pp. 154–5).

Spinal recovery position

a

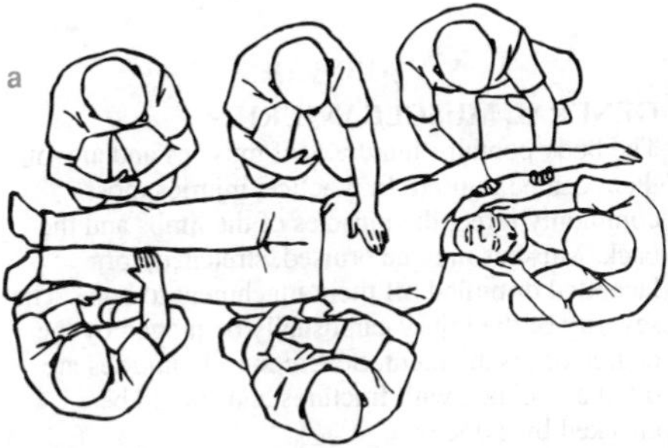

Spinal recovery position (continued)

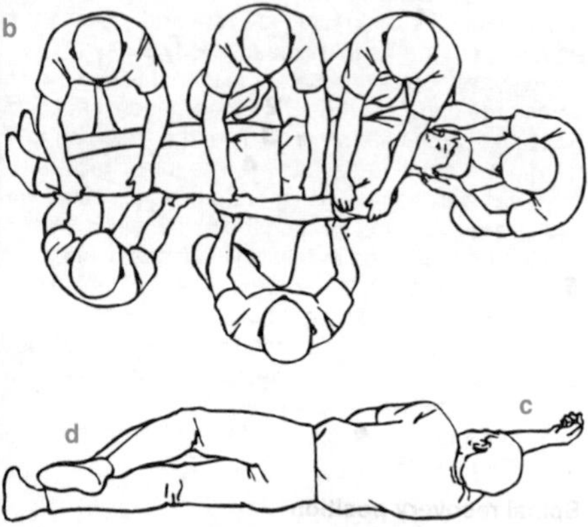

Muscle injuries

GENERAL MUSCLE INJURIES

The body contains hundreds of muscles and any of them can be injured. In practice, injuries most commonly affect the muscles of the limbs and the back. Muscles may be bruised, stretched, torn, lacerated or pulled off their attachment to bone. The severity of the injury can usually be judged by the degree of disablement. Severe muscle injuries are often associated with fractures and should be checked by a doctor.

Features

- Pain and tenderness when the injured part is pressed.
- Bruising, swelling and stiffness.
- Cramps may occur.
- Loss of the affected muscle's ability to function.

Management of muscle injuries

1 Sit or lay the injured person down. **2** Put the injured part in the most comfortable position. If the affected part is a limb, elevate it. **3** Apply a cold pack (ice-pack or a pack of frozen food, such as peas) (**a**), bandage it in place and leave for half an hour. This will limit internal bleeding and bruising. **4** Firmly compress the injured part with a thick layer of cotton wool bound on with a bandage (**b**). This will help to reduce swelling.

Muscle injuries

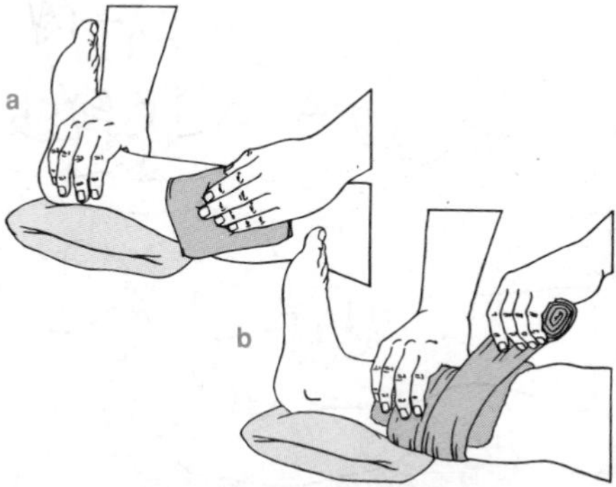

CRAMP

Cramp is a sudden, involuntary, tense, sustained contraction of a muscle or of several associated muscles. Such contractions are usually very painful. They may follow strenuous exercise or may occur at rest. They most commonly involve the calf muscles. Any muscle can, however, suffer cramp. In most cases, the cause is unknown but cramps frequently occur in very hot conditions if the victim has been sweating excessively. They may also be brought on by exercising in the cold, as in sea bathing. Most cramps will pass off within a few minutes, but pain can be very severe.

Relieving cramp

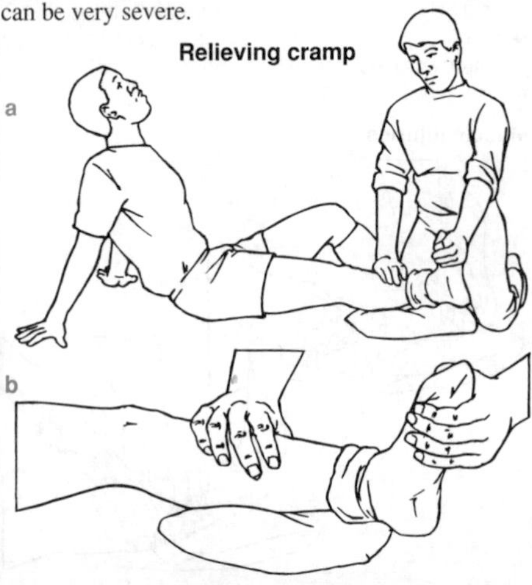

Features

- Pain.
- Tense bunching up of the affected muscles.
- Involuntary bending of toes or fingers.

Toe-, ankle- and finger-bending muscles

Most of the muscles that cause toe and ankle bending are in the lower leg. Most of those that bend the fingers are in the forearm. Quinine tablets are often helpful for night cramps.

Relieving cramp

1 Gently straighten any joint that is bent by the cramping muscles (**a**). **2** Gently massage the affected muscles (**b**).

Poisoning

GENERAL POISONING

How poisoning occurs

Poisoning may be suicidal, accidental or, rarely, homicidal. Attempts at suicide by poisoning are common and the circumstances often make it obvious what has happened. Alcohol is commonly used with other means of self-poisoning. Children are sometimes accidentally poisoned when they eat attractive-looking tablets or capsules, taking them for sweets. Accidental poisoning may also occur when dangerous liquids are stored in bottles that normally contain beverages. It can also arise when intravenous drug users experiment with dosage.

How poisons enter and affect the body

Poisonous substances may be eaten, drunk, inhaled, injected or absorbed through the skin. There are many thousands of different poisons and they act in various ways. Many of them interfere with biochemical (enzyme) systems in the body cells so that vital bodily processes, such as the utilization of oxygen, are stopped.

Features

These vary with the poison.

- Drowsiness or coma (narcotics).
- Abdominal pain, vomiting and diarrhoea (intestinal irritants).
- Salivating, weeping and pupils of the eyes contract (organophosphates, e.g. weedkillers and insecticides).
- Burning around the lips and in the mouth (corrosive poisons; e.g. bleach).
- Muscle spasms and arching of the back (strychnine).
- Convulsions (nervous system stimulants).
- Sweating and overbreathing (aspirin).
- Hypothermia (see pp. 127–8) (antipsychotic drugs and barbiturates).
- Pink skin (carbon monoxide).
- Skin blisters (anti-depressants and carbon monoxide).

Common poisons

- Insecticides and weedkillers.
- Organic and inorganic mercurial fungicides.
- Rat and mouse poisons.
- Corrosive agents, such as acids, alkalis, bleaches and disinfectants.
- Methylated spirits in small dosage.
- Drinking alcohol in large dosage.
- Rubbing alcohol.

- Antifreeze.
- Gases or vapours such as carbon monoxide, cyanides and hydrocarbons, e.g. paraffin.
- A wide range of drugs of all kinds, especially painkillers, antidepressants and benzodiazepines (see pp. 251–3).
- Various plants and fungi (see pp. 164–5).

Common poisons

Poisons found in the home

The most dangerous substances are the corrosive poisons used for the most difficult cleaning tasks. These are unlikely to be taken accidentally. Harmful household poisons include:

- ammonia;
- liquid bleach;
- toilet bowl cleaning powder or liquid;
- fungicides;

- oven cleaning liquids and sprays;
- rust removers;
- paint-strippers;
- spot removers, especially if inhaled;
- sterilizing fluids;
- various liquid glues, if inhaled.

Other household substances that are less dangerous but are still capable of doing harm, include:

- washing-up liquids;
- window cleaners;
- carpet cleaners;
- floor cleaners.

Poisons used in the garden

The organophosphate weedkillers and insecticides are particularly dangerous and can cause death or serious permanent damage to the lungs. All such substances should be treated with great respect and stored in such a way that they do not offer danger to children or inexperienced persons. They must always be clearly labelled and marked 'poison'. They should never be stored in containers that normally hold food or beverages. When they are used, suitable precautions must be taken to protect the skin and the eyes, and to avoid inhalation. Exposed parts of the body should be thoroughly washed after using any of these substances.

Poisonous plants and fungi

Several common plants are poisonous – some dangerously so. The general rule is simple – never eat any part of a plant growing in the garden or countryside unless you know precisely what it is and that it is commonly eaten. Distinctions are not always easy. The poisonous death cap mushroom *Amanita phalloides*, for instance, quite closely resembles some species of edible mushroom. This species accounts for 90 per cent of all mushroom poisoning deaths in Britain.

Common poisonous seeds, berries and fungi

- Laburnum seed pod (**a**).
- Deadly nightshade berries (**b**).
- Common ink-cap mushroom.
- Death cap mushroom (**c**).
- 'Magic' mushrooms.
- Deadly fly agaric mushroom (**d**).
- Yew (**e**).

Poisonous seeds, berries and fungi: examples

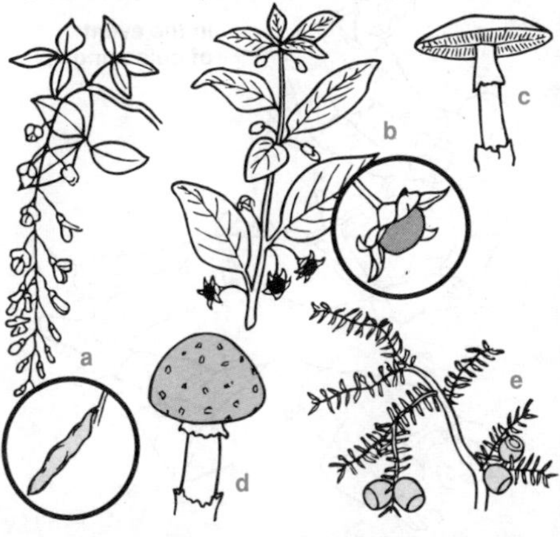

In the event of poisoning

1 Telephone for an ambulance immediately. **2** Get as much information from the victim as possible, including the name of the poison and the time it was swallowed. **3** If there are signs of burning of the mouth, make the victim drink a glass of water or milk slowly, but only if conscious (**a**). **4** Place in the recovery position (**b**) (see pp. 31–3), whether the victim is conscious or unconscious. **5** Collect the bottle/container/plant that the poison came from (**c**), and a sample of vomit (if any) for analysis by the medical professionals. **6** Get the victim to hospital as quickly as possible.

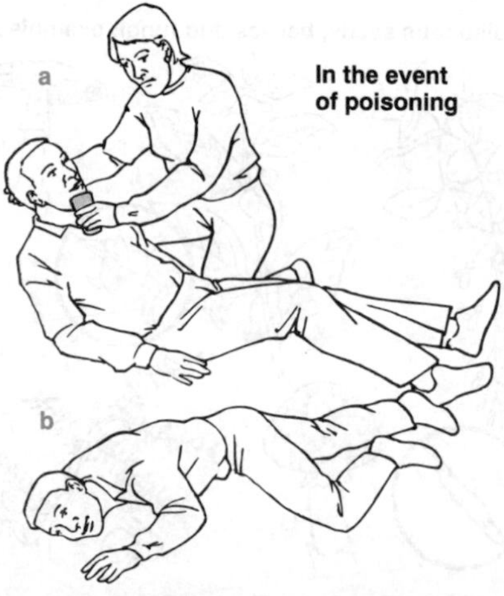

In the event of poisoning

✘ **Do not waste time** looking for antidotes.
✘ **Do not try** to cause vomiting.
♦ **If the victim is unconscious**, check for breathing (see pp. 17–18) and pulse (see p. 21).
♦ **If there is no breathing and no pulse**, give the victim artificial ventilation (see pp. 23–4) and external chest compression (see pp. 25–8).
✘ **When giving artificial ventilation**, make sure that the mouth is thoroughly cleaned of poison or use mouth-to-nose ventilation (**d**) (see p. 24).

c

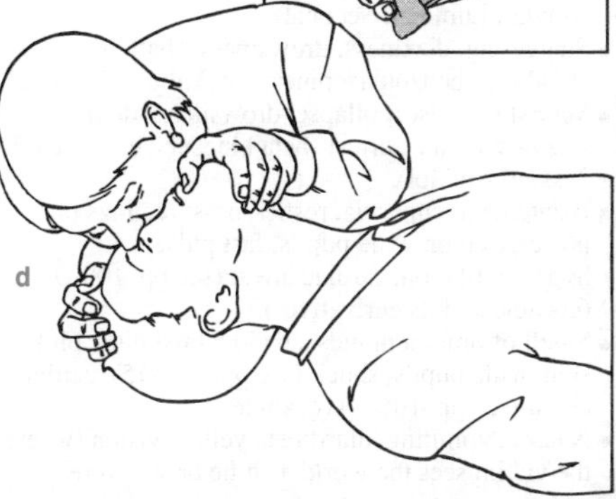
d

DRUG OVERDOSE

This is usual in an attempted suicide, but occasionally it is the result of misinterpretation of medical instructions or, rarely, because of a mistake in prescription or dispensing. Certain drugs are taken in overdose more often than others.

Features

Various effects of drug overdose are listed below, with the drugs responsible given in brackets.

- Jumpiness, excitement, confusion, aggression, hallucinations (amphetamines; e.g. Benzedrine, Dexedrine).
- Unconsciousness, ranging from sleep to deep, irreversible coma (narcotics; e.g. heroin, morphine, Codeine, Meperidine, Propoxyphene).
- Drowsiness, coma, hypothermia (see pp. 127–8), slow and shallow breathing (barbiturates; e.g. Amytal, Luminal, Seconal).
- Staggering, dizziness, drowsiness, shallow breathing (benzodiazepines; e.g. Valium, Librium).
- Very slow pulse, collapse, drowsiness, delirium, seizures, cardiac arrest (beta blockers; e.g. Sectral, Visken, Angilol).
- Excitement, euphoria, restlessness, feelings of power, tremor, wide pupils, fast pulse, hyperventilation, cardiac arrest (see pp. 108–9) (cocaine and its derivatives).
- Smell of bitter almonds, shallow breathing, pink skin, wide pupils, shock (see pp. 113–15), cardiac arrest (see pp. 108–9) (cyanide).
- Nausea, vomiting, diarrhoea, yellow vision (where the victim sees the world as if he or she were

looking through yellow glasses), slow irregular pulse (digitalis heart drug; e.g. Lanoxin).

- Abdominal pain, nausea, vomiting, rapid pulse, black stools (iron; e.g. Ferrocap, Ferromyn).
- Nausea, vomiting, apathy, tremor, muscle twitching, convulsions (lithium; e.g. Camcolit, Priadel).
- Nausea, vomiting, abdominal pain, headache, rapid breathing, disorientation, jerking movement of the eyes, seizures, drowsiness, coma, cardiac arrest (see pp. 108–9) (non-steroidal anti-inflammatory drugs [NSAIDs]; e.g. Brufen, Ebufac).
- Nausea and vomiting (paracetamol; e.g. Panadol). With paracetamol, acute liver failure, which is often fatal, may occur after 36 hours.
- Deafness, ringing in the ears, blurring of vision, profuse sweating, cardiac arrest. Coma in children (salicylates; e.g. aspirin).
- Dry mouth, wide pupils, inability to urinate, hallucinations, twitching, loss of consciousness (see pp. 173–5) (anti-depressants; e.g. Tofranil, Tryptizol).

In the event of drug overdose

See pp. 166–7.

✘ **Do not attempt** to keep the victim awake with black coffee or exercise. This will quicken the body's absorption of the drug.

ALCOHOL POISONING

This is very much a matter of degree. The term 'intoxication', literally and justifiably, means 'poisoning' but moderate degrees of intoxication do not normally require to be treated as cases of poisoning. If there is any doubt, however, drunkenness should be treated as seriously as any other kind of poisoning. Unfortunately, this is not widely appreciated and, because they were left lying on their backs, many heavily drunk people have died from inhaling their own vomit.

Features

- There is partial or total loss of consciousness.
- Breathing is deep.
- Vomiting.
- Flushing and sweating.
- The victim smells of drink.

✖ **Do not jump** to conclusions. Hypoglycaemia (see pp. 118–19) and overdoses of other drugs show some similarities to drunkeness.

In the event of alcohol poisoning

1 Open the airway (**a**) and check breathing (see pp. 18–20 and 17–18). **2** Check pulse (**b**) (see p. 21). **3** Check for injuries. **4** Place in the recovery position (**c**) (see pp. 31–3). **5** Check later for deterioration. **6** Send for an ambulance, if there is continuing cause for concern.

Alcohol poisoning

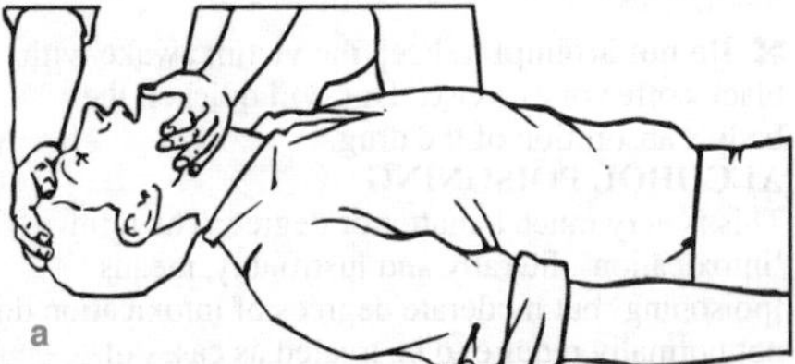
a

Alcohol poisoning (continued)

b

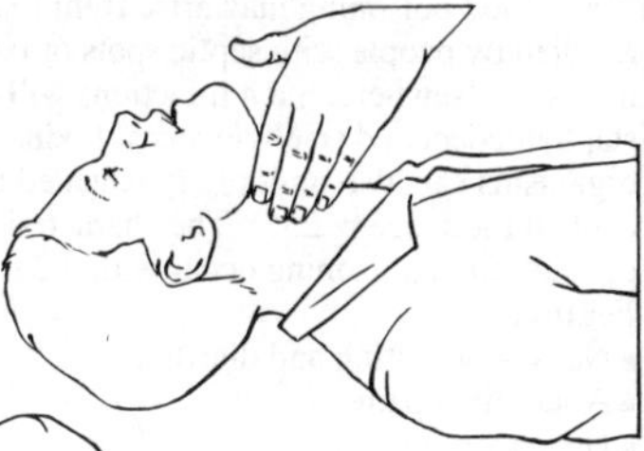

c

FOOD POISONING

Most cases of food poisoning are caused either by lack of hygiene on the part of food handlers or by the inadequate cooking of food. Food handlers who do not wash properly after using the toilet may pass on bowel organisms that can cause intestinal upset and may also pass on the hepatitis A virus. Most attacks of food poisoning are over after two or three days.

There are two types of bacteria that cause food poisoning: staphylococci and salmonella.

Acute (staphylococcal) food poisoning

Acute food poisoning may arise from food being handled by people with septic spots or boils on their hands or elsewhere. Such infections will contain staphylococci and staphylococcal toxins. The organisms can also multiply in reheated or half-cooked food (see p. 255). The characteristic features of acute food poisoning occur within 2 to 6 hours.

Features

- Nausea, vomiting and diarrhoea.
- Abdominal pain.
- Headache.
- Shock (see p. 113) is a possibility.

Salmonella poisoning

Salmonella poisoning is generally less acute and may take a day or two to develop.

Features

- Nausea, vomiting and diarrhoea.
- Abdominal pain.
- Headache.
- Fever.
- Shock (see p. 113) is a possibility.

Food poisoning

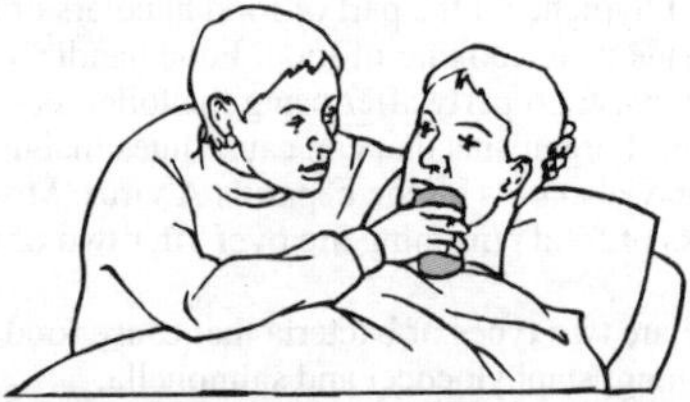

In the event of food poisoning

1 Give the victim plenty of water to drink. **2** Once the stomach has settled for a few hours, give jelly, blancmange, dry biscuits or clear soup.

✘ **Do not give** the victim food, milky drinks, tea, coffee or acidic drinks, such as fruit juices or squashes.

♦ **If there is abdominal pain**, blood in the stools or if symptoms are severe and last longer than three days, call a doctor.

Unconsciousness

Real harm will never be done by trying to rouse an apparently unconscious person in the manner described below. It is important to distinguish unconciousness from sleep.

Checking for unconsciousness

Check first whether there is any response to normal speech and whether the response is rational.

♦ **If there is no response**, try loud speech close to an ear. Check the effect of asking the victim to move the arms and legs, open the eyes, and so on.

♦ **If there is still no response**, check the reaction to pain.

Checking the reaction to pain

1 Press the point of the knuckle hard against the middle of the breastbone. **2** Move it a little up and down.

♦ **If this elicits no response**, such as a protest or a groan, the person is likely to be fairly deeply unconscious. ►►

Helping an unconscious person

1 Establish that the victim is unconscious (see p. 173). **2** Check for breathing (**a**) (see pp. 17–18). **3** Check the pulse (**b**) (see p. 21). **4** Check for injuries, especially head injuries, and give immediate first aid (see pp. 37–8), if appropriate. **5** Check for other possible causes of coma, such as needle marks (from injections of insulin or narcotics) or breath smelling like nail varnish or pear drops. **6** Check for medical identification, such as cards or bracelets (**c**) (diabetes, epilepsy, steroid medication, etc.). **7** If injuries allow, place the victim

Helping an unconscious person

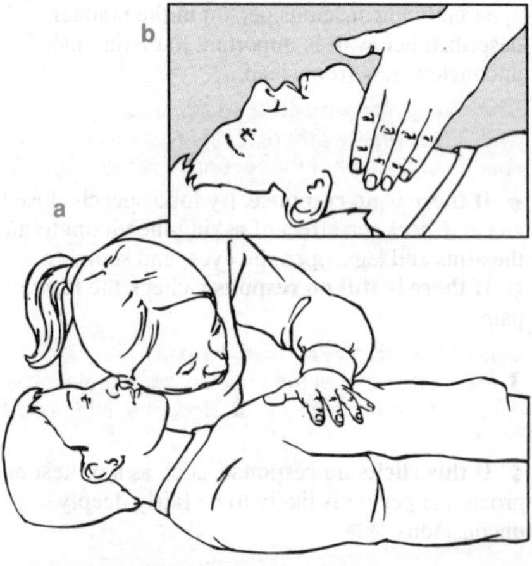

in the recovery position (**d**) (see pp. 31–3).
8 Loosen tight clothing. **9** Send for medical help.

✖ **Do not leave** the victim alone.

◆ **If it is not possible** to place the victim in the recovery position, keep a constant check on the airway.

◆ **If there is any immediate risk** of airway obstruction, e.g. from vomiting, it may be necessary to turn the victim on to his or her side even if a spinal injury is suspected (see p. 58).

c

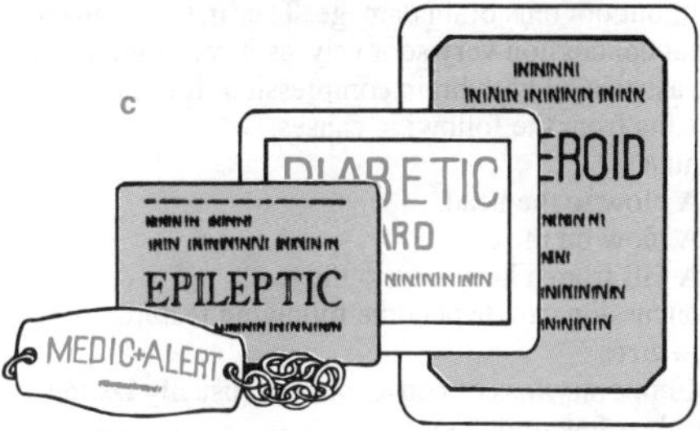

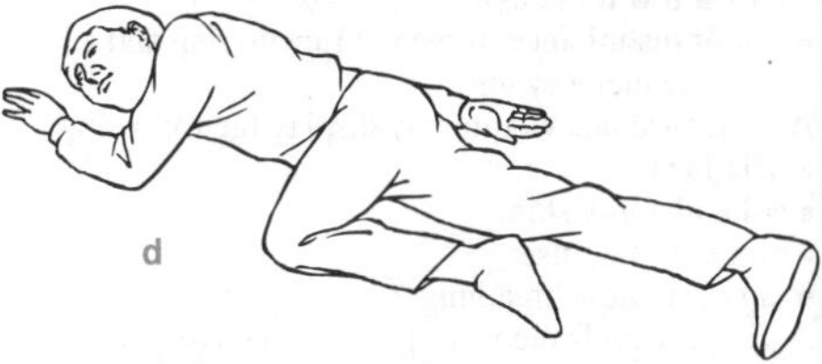

d

HEAD INJURIES

Injuries to the head may cause damage to the brain which can result in concussion or compression. Such damage can mask associated injuries to the abdomen, chest, limbs or spine. It is therefore necessary to give the victim a thorough preliminary examination (see pp. 17–21 and 37–8).

See pp. 150–1 or 201–2 if the victim has suffered a skull fracture or scalp wound.

Concussion

Concussion is a disordered state of consciousness without obvious brain damage. The first aider must treat concussion very seriously, as it can sometimes be associated with brain compression. It usually results from the following causes.

Causes

- A blow to the head.
- A blow on the chin.
- A fall from a height on to the feet.

Concussion can display the following features.

Features

- Temporary loss of consciousness (usually lasting only a few minutes).
- Minor disturbance of mental functioning and possible memory loss.

An unconscious victim may display the following:

- pale face;
- cold, clammy skin;
- rapid, weak pulse;
- rapid, shallow breathing.

A victim who is recovering from concussion can sometimes feel nauseated and may be vomiting.

Management of concussion

1 Carry out general treatment for unconsciousness, if necessary. **2** Watch carefully for signs of compression, even after apparent recovery. **3** Arrange removal to hospital.

Brain compression

Compression can immediately follow concussion (with no return to consciousness), or can occur up to two days after apparent recovery.

It is caused by pressure exerted on some part of the brain by a depressed fracture of the skull, or by fluid or blood within the skull. As a result, the brain may be forced downwards, so that vital centres in the brainstem may be destroyed, with fatal results.

Compression usually displays most of the following features.

Features

- Deepening unconsciousness.
- Twitching of limbs, or even convulsions.
- Noisy breathing.
- High body temperature, with flushed face and slow pulse.
- The pupils of the eyes become abnormal. They may: become unequal in size; both be dilated; or fail to react to light.
- Weakness or paralysis on one side of the body.

Management of compression

Get the victim to hospital as quickly as possible.

♦ **If the victim's alertness** and level of consciousness fall as compression develops, then urgent medical attention will be required.

Wound infection

The surface of the skin, however clean, always contains infective organisms, and normal daily living constantly brings us into contact with more of these organisms. Normal faeces consist largely of infective organisms and often contain dangerous germs. It is impossible to wipe the bottom without contaminating the fingers. Hot, sweaty, unexposed skin areas, such as the feet, groin and armpits, commonly become infected unless washed daily. Good personal hygiene, based on an appreciation of these facts, will help avoid spontaneous skin infection. It will not prevent infection if the surface of the skin is breached by a cut or abrasion. It will, however, lessen the probability and severity of infection of a clean wound.

Infection causes inflammation, which can display the following features.

Features

- Redness.
- Heat.
- Swelling.
- Throbbing.
- Pain.
- Some loss of function.

Preventing wound infection

1 Wash wounds thoroughly using gauze swabs and soap (**a**). Dirt, cloth, foreign material and dead tissue must – as far as possible – be removed. **2** Dry with a sterile swab or allow to dry by evaporation. **3** Cover with a sterile dressing.

The dressing must be securely fixed (**b**): it will have to remain in place until the wound has healed.

✖ **Avoid contamination** by always wiping away from the wound and constantly changing the swab, so as not to move from dirty skin back to the wound.

✖ **Do not re-contaminate**, after cleaning, by drying with a used towel.

◆ **If a wound becomes infected**, seek medical advice.

Preventing wound infection

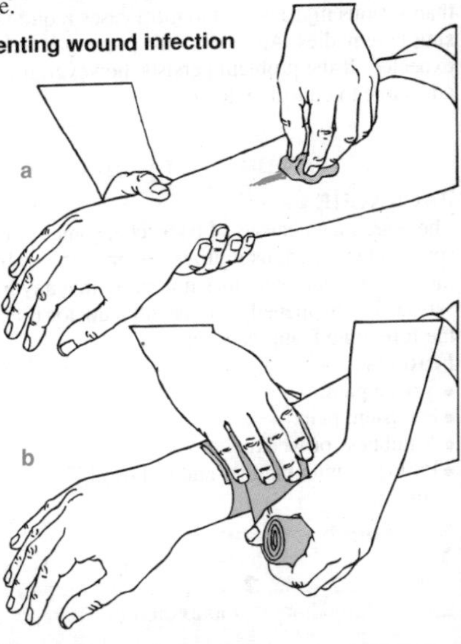

4. Minor injuries and conditions

Many of the conditions dealt with in this section of the book are not serious enough to warrant medical attention. Some of them, however, can be potentially dangerous, and these always require medical attention. Minor injuries are far more common than serious injuries, and in most cases require only simple remedies. As a rule, full recovery is to be expected. If the problem persists, however, it is advisable to consult a doctor.

Aches and pains

BACKACHE

There are many causes of backache, some serious, some not (for serious injuries see pp. 155–8). In most cases back pain does not imply that anything serious has happened, but consult a doctor if any of the following features occur.

Features

- Severe pain.
- Persistent pain.
- Numbness or weakness in a leg.
- Problems with bladder and/or bowel control.

Relieving backache

1 Apply local heat to the back from a hot-water bottle or heat lamp. **2** Use painkilling drugs such as aspirin, paracetamol or ibuprofen for short periods.

Relieving backache

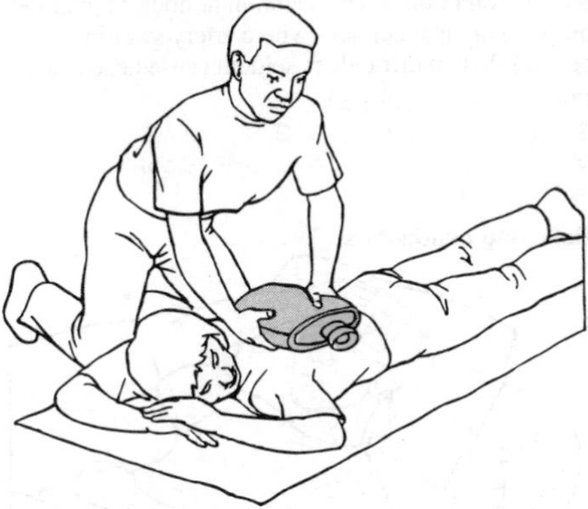

◆ **If the pain does not settle** in a day or two, consult a doctor.

HEADACHE

The great majority of headaches are caused by muscle tension responding in turn to psychological tension. There are also other, less frequent, causes of headaches.

Causes

- Excessive alcohol consumption.
- Hunger.
- Tiredness.
- Oppressive weather.
- Migraine.
- Allergies.

Only a very small proportion of headaches indicate a serious condition, such as a brain tumour, high blood pressure or an aneurysm (where artery swelling occurs). Visual difficulties seldom cause headaches.

Relieving headaches

1 The victim should relax. **2** Use painkillers.
3 Apply a cold compress or covered hot-water bottle to the forehead.

Relieving headaches

Headaches occurring for no obvious reason

Such headaches should be reported and investigated. This is particularly important in the case of headaches associated with other symptoms, such as weakness or loss of sensation, or loss of parts of the field of vision.

EARACHE

This is particularly common in children, in whom it is usually due to infection in the middle ear (**a**) or in the passage (**b**) leading to the ear drum (**c**). Other cases may be due to a small boil in the ear passage.

Section through the ear

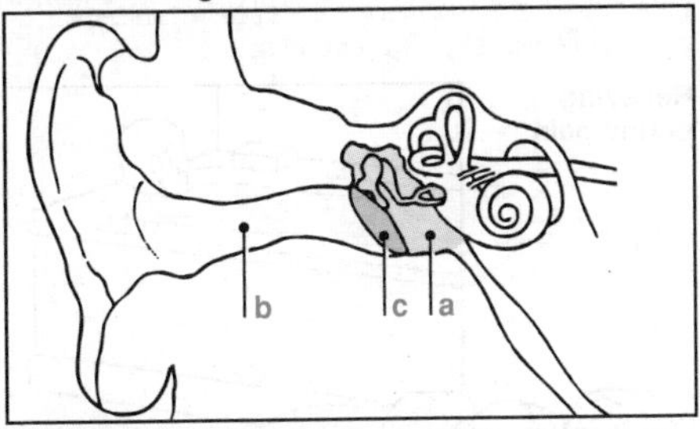

Consult a doctor if any of the following features are present.

Features

- Fever.
- Deafness.
- Discharge from the ear.

Relieving earache

1 Self-help is limited to giving painkilling drugs.

2 Check the victim's temperature and consult a doctor if a fever is developing.

◆ **If the pain persists** for more than a day, consult a doctor.

✖ **Avoid giving aspirin to children** under 12. Use paracetamol in suitable dosage.

PERIOD PAIN

Painful periods are very common and do not usually imply anything very serious.

Relieving period pain

1 Use painkillers such as ibuprofen, aspirin or codeine. **2** When the pain is particularly severe, take a hot bath and then relax for a time in bed, preferably with a hot-water bottle.

Relieving period pain

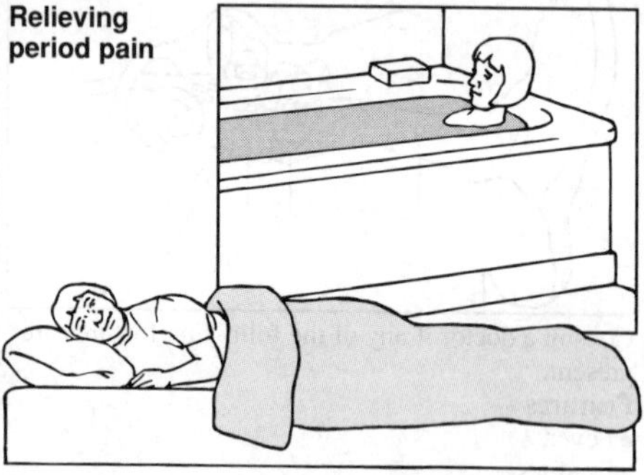

◆ **If the pain is very severe and persistent**, consult a doctor – it may be due to serious disorders, such as pelvic infection or hormone imbalance, or to some other gynaecological problem.

The combined oral contraceptive pill

In many cases, the contraceptive pill is an effective way of treating very severe period pains. This is because it prevents egg production (ovulation): cycles without ovulation are always painless.

SINUS PAIN

Acute sinusitis commonly follows a cold and causes pain – often throbbing – above, below or between the eyes. The pain may be associated with fever, in which case medical attention is advised.

Location of the sinuses

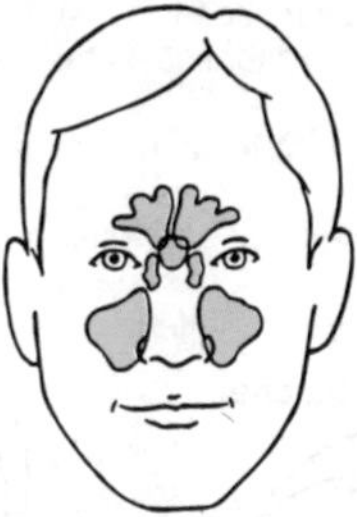

Methods of relieving sinus pain

1 Use decongestant nose drops or a decongestant nasal spray. It is often helpful to inhale the vapour from hot water in a bowl, with a towel over the head.

2 Tincture of benzoin inhalations are also commonly used for sinusitis. They are available without prescription.

TOOTHACHE

Toothache is pain occurring in the jaws or teeth, which may be continuous, intermittent or throbbing. There are several different causes of toothache.

Causes

- Dental decay, with infection of the tooth pulp (**a**; see overleaf).
- Exposure of sensitive dentine at the necks of the teeth.

- Deep, unlined fillings.
- Tooth fractures.

Methods of relieving toothache

There are several ways to relieve toothache.

1 If sharp toothache occurs on contact with acids, fruits or ice-cream, it can probably be relieved by using a toothpaste that seals the tubules in the dentine (**b**).

2 The affected tooth can be dabbed with oil of cloves (**c**).

3 The victim can place a covered hot-water bottle against the painful side of the face.

4 Painkillers may be taken.

Relieving toothache

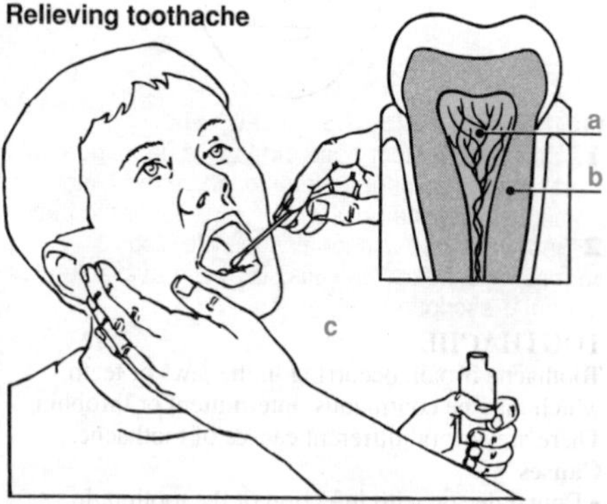

◆ **If there is still pain** the victim should see a dentist without delay as the pulp (**a**) of the affected tooth may be infected.

Bites and stings

DOG, CAT AND HUMAN BITES

Animal and human mouths contain large numbers of organisms, some capable of producing serious infections and even potentially fatal diseases, such as rabies. Bites that penetrate the skin must, therefore, always be taken seriously.

Management of bites

1 Immediately wash the bite well with plenty of soap and water. **2** Allow the bite to bleed naturally, in order to carry away germs. **3** Apply gauze soaked in hydrogen peroxide, in order to reduce the risk of infection. **4** Report the bite to a doctor, as tetanus immunization and antibiotics may be required. **5** If rabies is suspected, the victim must be taken to hospital.

Verification of rabies

In order to verify or exclude a rabies infection, a suspect animal must undergo medical examination. Attempt to isolate the animal only if it is possible to do so safely. If a suspect animal escapes, inform the police at once.

SNAKEBITES

Snakebites are rare in Britain and are seldom serious, hardly ever causing death. The adder is the only poisonous species in Britain and about 100 people sustain adder bites each year. In other parts of the world, other types of snake, such as vipers, cobras, kraits, coral snakes and mambas, are common and cause many deaths.

The medical authorities in areas of high prevalence

of poisonous snakes hold stocks of antivenom and are experienced in the management of snakebites.

Features

- There is pain and swelling around the bite.
- One or two puncture wounds are evident.
- The victim's vision may deteriorate.
- There is nausea and there may be vomiting.
- There may be breathing difficulty.

Management of snakebites

1 The victim must be made to rest (**a**) in order to slow the heart down, thereby reducing poison absorption. **2** Clean the wound by wiping away from the bite (**b**), to remove any venom that may be around the wound. **3** Bandage the wound firmly (**c**). **4** Get the victim to a hospital or to a doctor as quickly as possible.

Management of snakebites

a

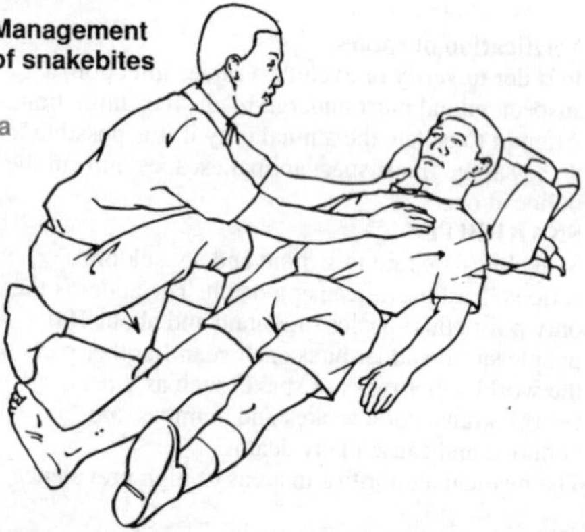

✖ **Do not let** the victim move.
✖ **Do not elevate** the injured limb.
✖ **Do not cut** into or cauterize the bite.

Management of snakebites (continued)

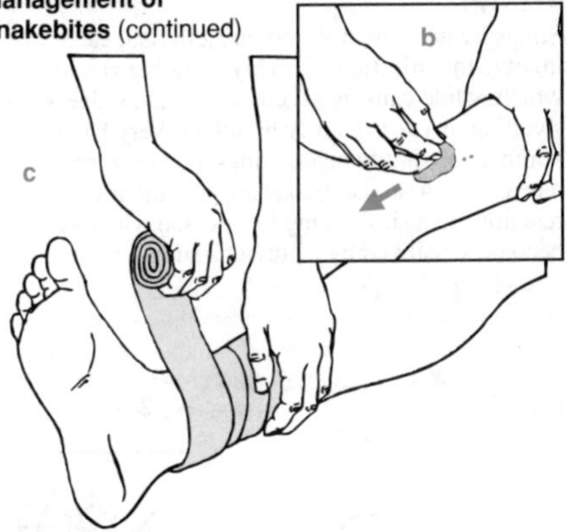

INSECT BITES

These are not really bites but are usually the effect of a small quantity of material in the insect's saliva, which is injected into the skin via the insect's proboscis. The material causes an allergic reaction – taking the form of redness, swelling and irritation – which usually settles in a day or two. Some reactions are caused by insect faeces scratched into the skin. Occasionally, severe reactions occur which may be life-threatening, especially if swelling occurs in the voice-box (larynx).

Treating insect bites

1 Wash the skin area thoroughly with soap and water. **2** All severe local or general reactions should be reported to a doctor without delay.

STINGS

Stings by bees, wasps, hornets, jellyfish, etc., involve the injection of highly irritating venom, which, while causing severe local pain, redness and swelling, is usually fairly harmless. Very large numbers of simultaneous stings, however, may be dangerous. Also dangerous are general allergic reactions to a single sting in a person who has become sensitized by a previous sting.

Treating stings

1 Sting sacs left protruding from the skin must be carefully scraped off with a blunt knife blade (**a**) or a fingernail. **2** Wash the affected area with soap and water (**b**) and apply an ice cube (**c**). **3** Administer painkillers to the victim.

Treating stings

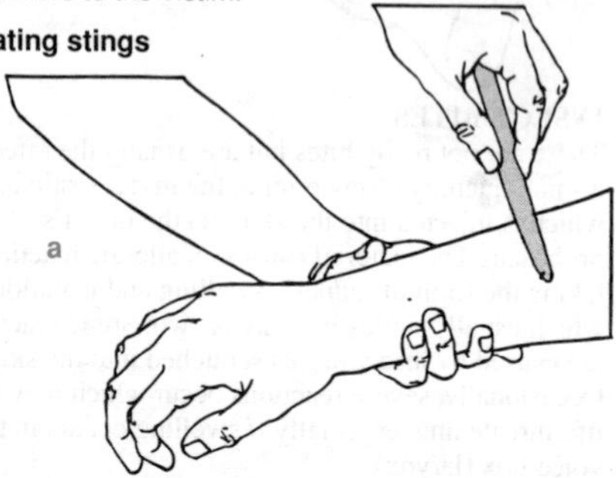

Treating stings (continued)

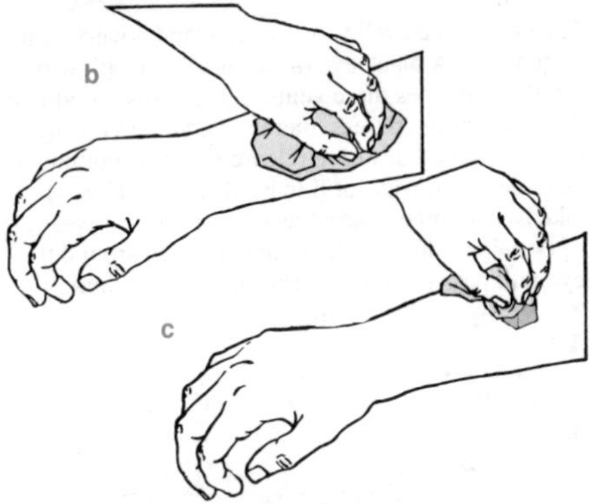

✘ **Avoid using tweezers** to remove the sting, as this will squeeze the venom into the skin.

Stings in the mouth or throat

In this instance, the victim must be taken to a doctor or hospital casualty department immediately. Such stings may cause fatal swelling of the voice-box with obstruction of the airway.

General allergic reactions

Any general allergic reactions require immediate medical attention.

If a person collapses after a sting

1 Check the breathing (see pp. 17–18). **2** Check the pulse (see p. 21). **3** Perform mouth-to-mouth artificial ventilation (see pp. 23–4) and chest compression (see p. 26–8), if necessary.

Black eye

The skin of the eyelids is very thin and covers many large veins. A black eye (**a**) results from a blow or fall that damages these veins and releases blood into the surrounding tissues, thereby darkening the area. Once the blood has been released there is nothing to be done but to wait for it to be absorbed. This will take two to three weeks (depending on the severity of bruising), during which time the skin around the eye will pass through a series of varied colours.

Treating a black eye

1 Place an ice pack (such as a pack of frozen peas) on the eye area (**b**) immediately after the injury has been sustained, in order to minimize its prominence. **2** Check the vision in the affected eye as soon as possible. **3** If vision seems impaired, then the victim's eyelids should be pulled slightly open with fingers (**c**) and the vision compared with that of the other eye. **4** The eyes should be moved from side to side and up and down to check for double vision.

A black eye

a

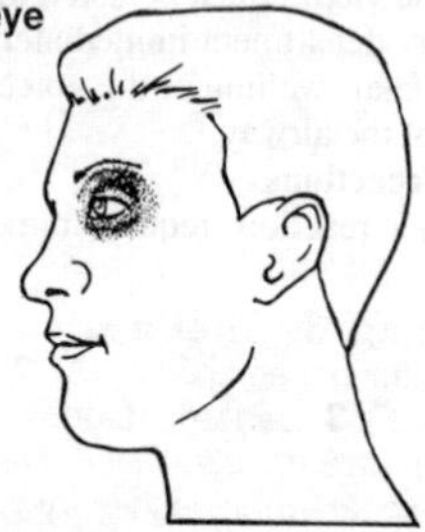

A black eye (continued)

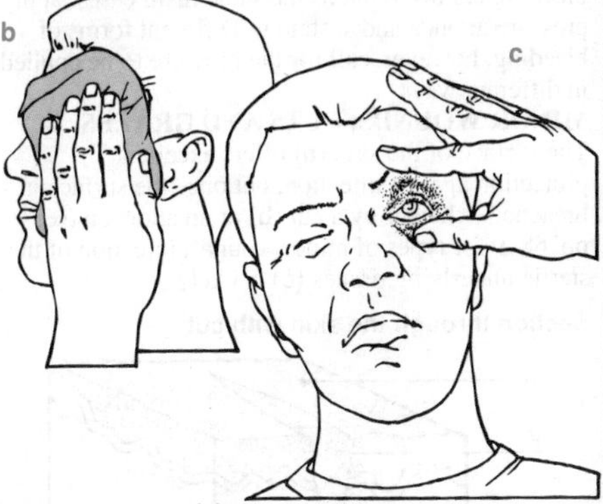

Problems with vision
Consult a doctor immediately if there is any visual problem of any kind.

Bleeding

Minor bleeding seldom presents any serious problems unless the person concerned is suffering from a bleeding disorder, such as haemophilia. Minor bleeding always results from damage to small blood vessels, such as venules (small veins) or capillaries. Pulsating spurts of bright red blood from an artery, however small, can never be considered minor and will always require medical attention (see pp. 34–5 and 70–3).

The principle behind the various methods of bleeding control remains the same in all cases: apply pressure at once and sustain it. Different forms of bleeding, however, call for the pressure to be applied in different ways.

MINOR WOUNDS, CUTS AND GRAZES

The surface of the skin (**a**) offers excellent protection against infection, but once the surface is breached, whether by a cut (**b**) or an abrasion (see pp. 68–9 for types of minor wound), infection of the sterile underlying tissues (**c**) is likely.

Section through the skin with cut

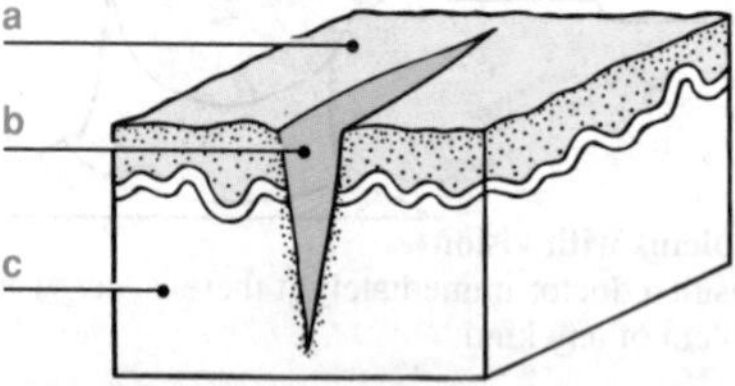

In most cases, the body's defence mechanisms can cope with any such infection, and the wound heals after a short period of inflammation. From time to time, however, minor cuts are contaminated with very dangerous (virulent) organisms, and serious infections, such as blood poisoning, may result.

Treating a minor wound

1 Wash the wound and the surrounding skin thoroughly with soap and water (**a**) as soon as a minor wound, cut or graze is sustained. **2** Remove any foreign material and dirt from the wound.

3 Wash hands, and then shake them dry. **4** Swab the skin around the wound with an antiseptic solution (**b**) (checking the instructions on the bottle for correct usage). **5** Apply a sterile dressing or 'plaster' (the sealed type of dressing, with plastic tabs that are pulled sideways to uncover the sterile surface) (**c**) after the wound has been thoroughly cleaned. Leave the dressing in place until the wound has healed. Disturb it only if it comes loose or becomes very dirty. ►►

Treating a minor wound

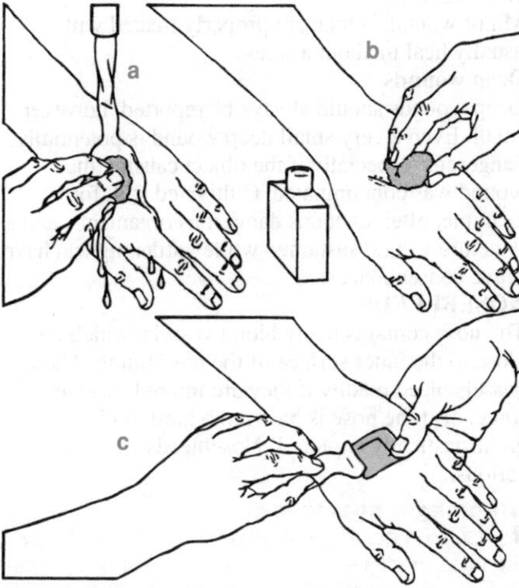

✘ **Do not touch the wound**, even with a clean towel.

✘ **Avoid touching the surface of the dressing** that comes in contact with the wound.

✘ **Do not use a towel for drying hands** unless it is newly laundered. Used towels carry germs which can contaminate the wound.

♦ **If the wound is still not comfortable** after the first day, and is accompanied by increasing pain, heat, swelling or throbbing, then a doctor must be consulted.

Healing time

Minor wounds which are properly treated will usually heal in about a week.

Deep wounds

Deep wounds should always be reported, however small. Even a very small deep wound is potentially dangerous, especially if the object causing the wound was contaminated. Cultivated soil, for example, often contains dangerous organisms, and a puncture wound sustained while gardening can have grave consequences.

NOSEBLEEDS

The nose contains many blood vessels, which lie close to the inner surface of the nose lining. These vessels bleed readily if they are injured by external force, or if the nose is blown too hard or over-enthusiastically explored! Nosebleeds are seldom serious.

Stopping a nosebleed

1 Pinch the nostrils in the area immediately below the nasal bones firmly with the thumb and forefinger (**a**) as soon as a nosebleed is recognized. **2** The victim should sit down with head forward over a washbowl (**b**). **3** The pressure on the bleeding vessels must be maintained for at least ten minutes, and the victim must not raise the head. **4** Release the pressure gradually. **5** With the head still forward, wipe carefully around the mouth and nose with a clean dressing or swab which has been soaked in lukewarm water (**c**). ►►

Stopping a nosebleed

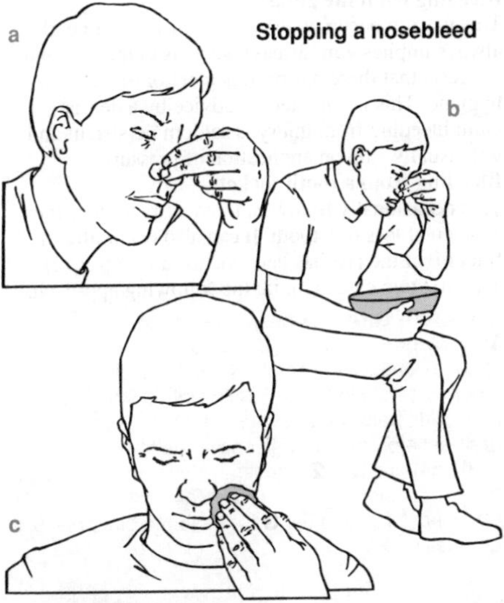

✖ **The victim must avoid blowing the nose** for at least four hours after the bleeding has stopped, if this is at all possible.

♦ **If the bleeding continues**, steps 1 to 5 should be repeated.

♦ **If the bleeding still continues**, then the victim must be taken to a hospital casualty department. The victim must still hold the nose.

GUM AND TOOTH SOCKET BLEEDING

Bleeding from the gums

This usually occurs while tooth-brushing; it nearly always implies gum disease, such as gingivitis, and suggests that there has been neglect of tooth hygiene. This is a matter for advice by a dentist. Gum bleeding from injury is seldom persistent and will usually stop on application of pressure.

Bleeding from a tooth socket

This occasionally follows a tooth extraction or the accidental loss of a tooth. It can also occur after a fracture of the jaw has been incurred (see p. 152). The first two cases require the following approach.

Stopping tooth socket bleeding

1 Apply pressure to the socket by means of a pad of some kind. Use a small, clean handkerchief, or other piece of clean cloth, rolled into a small cylinder that will fit between the teeth on either side of the gap, while protruding well above the level of the teeth margins (**a**). **2** Bite firmly on the cloth so as to force it against the socket (**b**). Maintain the pressure for at least 10 minutes. **3** Release the bite pressure gradually.

Stopping tooth socket bleeding

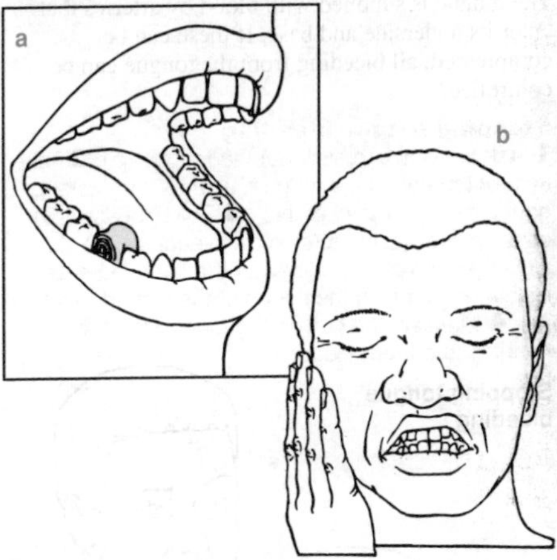

♦ **If the tooth socket continues to bleed**, it may be necessary to maintain the pressure for longer than this or to repeat the procedure.

✖ **Avoid pulling out any blood clot** that has formed by removing the cloth carefully.

♦ **If the blood clot still comes out**, try lubricating the cloth with a little sterile vaseline before putting it back in.

♦ **If this method still fails to stop the bleeding**, seek help from a dentist or a hospital casualty department.

TONGUE BLEEDING

The tongue is supplied with blood by arteries that enter its underside and base. If these can be compressed, all bleeding from the tongue can be controlled.

Stopping tongue bleeding

1 Ask the victim to stick out the tongue (**a**). **2** Take hold of the end of the tongue, using a clean cloth, gauze swab or handkerchief. **3** Pull it forward (**b**), as far as necessary to stop the bleeding, in order to kink the deep blood vessels. If the bleeding area is visible, try to press the edges of the wound together (**c**). **4** Maintain the pull on the tongue for about 10 minutes and then release it gently.

Stopping tongue bleeding

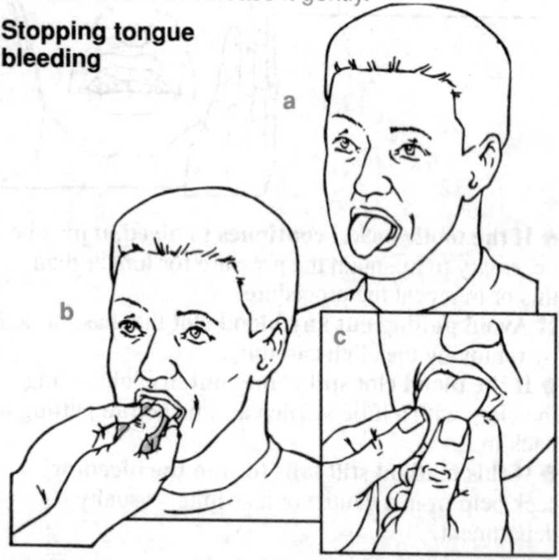

◆ **If the bleeding continues**, then repeat the procedure.
◆ **If the bleeding still continues**, then dental or medical aid is required.

Swallowing blood

Swallowing a little blood will do no harm. If swallowed blood is vomited, the victim requires hospital attention.

SCALP BLEEDING

The scalp is very well supplied with blood vessels and bleeds profusely, for a time, if cut. Anything more than the most minor of scalp cuts will require medical attention. A small cut, properly treated, will usually heal rapidly.

Stopping minor scalp bleeding

1 Small cuts must be thoroughly washed with soap and water (**a**), and all foreign material removed.
2 Press the edges of the wound together with the fingers (**b**; see overleaf). ►►

Stopping minor scalp bleeding

a

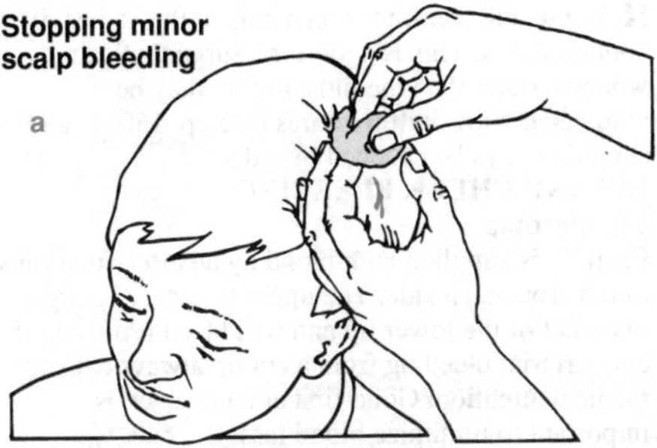

Stopping minor scalp bleeding (continued)

b

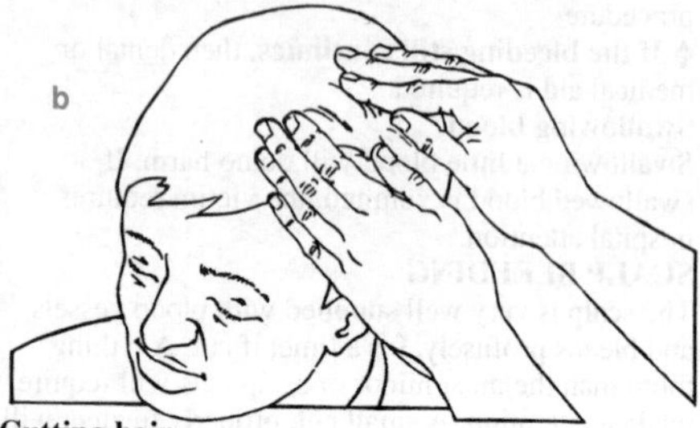

Cutting hair

If the victim's hair is obstructing treatment, it may be necessary to cut the hair for a centimetre or so around the wound (it will soon grow again), to ensure that the area can be properly cleaned up, and to avoid getting hair between the edges of the wound.

✘ **Avoid self-treatment** on a wound that is heavily contaminated. This is a job for a surgeon. Scalp wounds, other than the most minor, may be associated with skull fractures (see pp. 150–1) and should always be checked by a doctor.

LIP AND CHEEK BLEEDING

Lip bleeding

Each lip is supplied with blood by an artery that runs into it from each side. The upper lip artery is larger than that of the lower lip and will bleed profusely if cut. Arterial bleeding from a cut lip always calls for medical attention. Good first aid, however, is important to minimize blood loss.

Stopping lip bleeding

1 Pinch the edges of the lip wound together between finger and thumb. This is best done through a gauze swab, but until this or some suitable substitute (such as a clean handkerchief) can be obtained, you may have to pinch with the bare fingers. **2** Sustain the pressure until medical help is available, occasionally reducing it to see whether the bleeding has stopped.

Stopping lip bleeding

Cheek bleeding

A similar procedure can be used to control bleeding from a cut in the cheek, but in this case you may have to experiment a little to find the best area to compress.

BLEEDING VARICOSE VEINS

Bleeding from varicose veins is uncommon, but can be severe.

Controlling bleeding varicose veins

1 The victim should lie down. **2** The injured leg should be raised as high as possible (**a**).
3 Pressure should be applied to the bleeding area with a clean pad or handkerchief (**b**). **4** Keep the leg in this position and maintain the pressure for about five minutes, after which time bleeding will usually have stopped. **5** Secure the pad in place with a bandage (**c**) (see p. 231). **6** The victim must see a doctor.

Controlling bleeding varicose veins

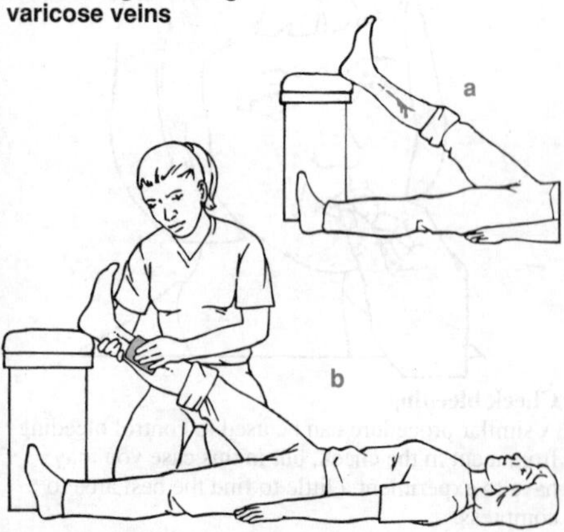

Controlling bleeding varicose veins (continued)

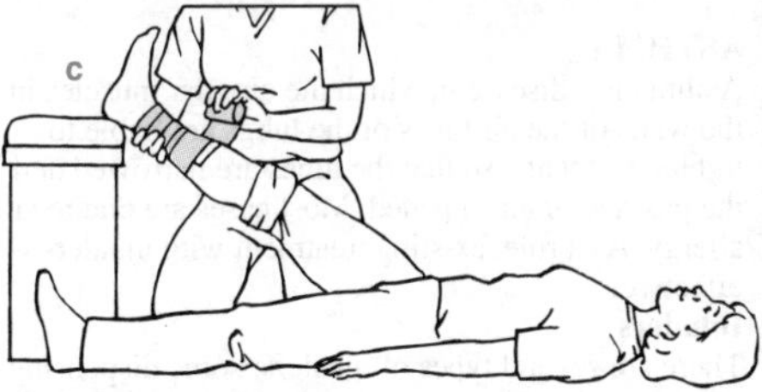

VAGINAL BLEEDING

Bleeding from the vagina, apart from menstrual bleeding, should always be taken seriously. Possible causes include threatened miscarriage in younger women and cancer in older women. Any vaginal bleeding which is not thought to be menstrual, and, in particular, any bleeding occurring after the menopause, should be reported without delay: nothing can be done by the first aider to stop severe vaginal bleeding, which must be considered as internal bleeding (see p. 73).

Preliminary management of vaginal bleeding

Minor vaginal bleeding can be managed as a normal menstrual period. Severe bleeding must be treated as a potential miscarriage.

Where miscarriage is suspected

1 Telephone for an ambulance. **2** The victim should lie down, with her feet raised. **3** Put a sanitary towel between her legs. **4** Treat for shock (see pp. 114–15), if bleeding is severe.

Breathing problems

ASTHMA

Asthma is a disease in which the circular muscles in the walls of the air tubes of the lungs are liable to tighten suddenly, so that the tubes are narrowed and the passage of air impeded. Most cases are due to an allergy. As a rule, existing treatment with inhalers is effective.

Inhalers

There are several types of inhalers, some dispensing a fine powder, others an aerosol spray of a solution of the medication.

Using an inhaler

The victim must ensure that the dose of medication enters the windpipe, and the air tubes of the lungs (bronchi), by synchronizing the release of the medication with a deep inhalation, so that the drug is carried well into the lungs.

♦ **If the asthma attack continues** then take the following course of action.

Management of severe asthma

1 Call an ambulance. **2** Try to calm the victim.
3 He or she should sit down, leaning forward slightly, resting the elbows on the back of a chair.
4 Open a window, unless the weather is cold.

✖ **Avoid any delay** in getting the victim to hospital.

HICCUPS

Hiccups occur as a result of involuntary diaphragm contractions. Most attacks stop quickly and do not require treatment.

Persistent hiccuping occurs only occasionally. It

results from organic disease and can continue for hours or even days.

Methods of stopping hiccups

A Hiccups can often be cured by activities which distract the victim's attention from the problem: determined breath-holding, up to the limit of endurance, will usually end an attack; and provoking a sneeze, by tickling the inside of a nostril, often proves effective.

B Another common treatment for hiccups is for the victim to drink water from the far side of a glass. The procedure for this is as follows. **1** Fill a normal glass with drinking water. **2** Place the lips over the side of the glass exactly opposite to the side from which one would normally drink (**a**). **3** Bend over in order to drink from the glass (**b**).

◆ **If the symptoms persist**, then the victim will require medical attention.

Hiccups

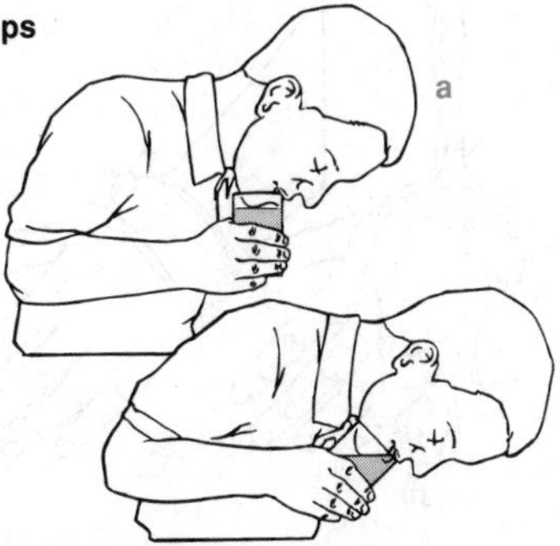

Burns

See pp. 92–5 for management of major burns.

MINOR BURNS AND SCALDS

Treating minor burns and scalds

1 All burns, however minor, should be treated by immediate cooling to minimize tissue damage. Get the injured part under a gushing cold tap (**a**) as quickly as possible, and keep it there until thoroughly cooled. **2** Dress the burn with clean, non-fluffy material (**b**) (see pp. 95 and 227–8) which is preferably sterile.

✘ **Do not interfere with the blister** by pricking it or removing any loose skin.

Treating minor burns and scalds

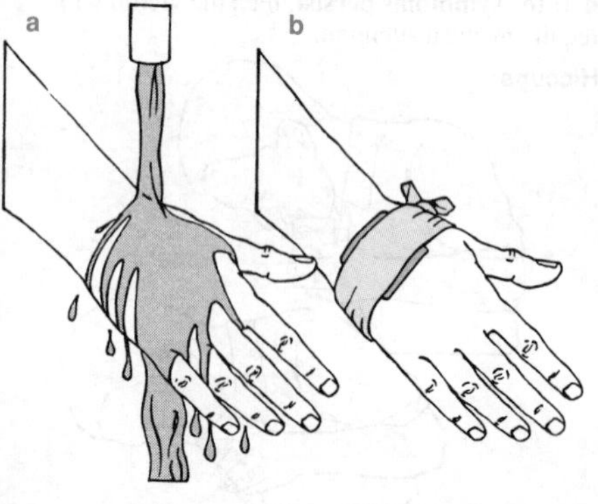

SUNBURN

Sunburn is caused by excessive exposure to the sun's rays. Sunlight contains ultraviolet rays which destroy cells in the outer layer of the skin and damage the small blood vessels which lie beneath the skin. Sunburn can vary from mild burning to severe blistering. It has two effects.

Effects

- Immediate discomfort and inconvenience.
- Long-term increase in the risk of skin wrinkling and skin cancer.

Relieving sunburn

1 Get out of the sun. **2** Cool the skin under a cold shower. **3** Avoid pressure on the burnt skin. **4** In cases of mild sunburn apply witch hazel, natural yoghurt, calamine lotion or a proprietary lotion or cream. **5** Try to preserve blisters in more serious cases. **6** Use painkillers. **7** Seek medical advice if burning is severe.

Relieving sunburn

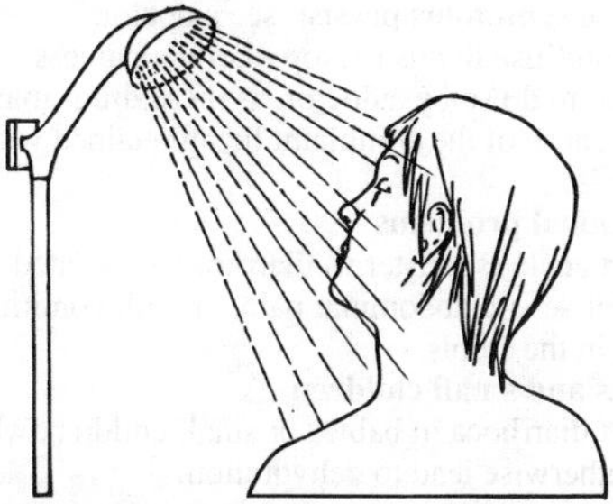

Diarrhoea

Diarrhoea is a common and usually brief complaint. Its symptoms are loose and liquid stools which are passed more frequently than normal. In most cases no treatment is needed as diarrhoea is itself a healing process.

Treating diarrhoea

Drink plenty of fluids (**a**) but avoid solid food (**b**) until the attack is over.

Treating diarrhoea

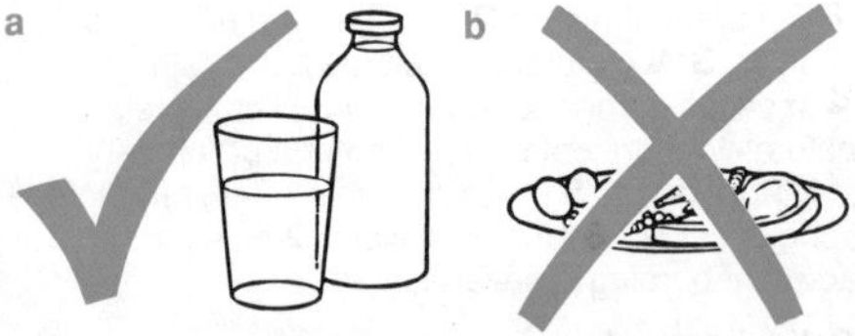

♦ **If the symptoms persist**, see a doctor.

✖ **Do not use drugs** to stop diarrhoea unless advised to do so by a doctor, as these drugs may lead to the cause of the complaint being retained within the body.

Additional problems

Report acute (short-term) diarrhoea associated with fever or severe abdominal pain, or with vomiting or blood in the stools.

Babies and small children

Report diarrhoea in babies or small children, which may otherwise lead to dehydration.

Extremes of body temperature

FROSTBITE

Frostbite is most dangerous when it causes the freezing of blood vessels, which can then cut off the blood supply to the affected area and may result in gangrene.
Extremities, such as the nose tip, the fingers and the toes, are most at risk. When frostbitten they initially become cold, hard and white, and then red and swollen.

Management of frostbite

1 Get the affected person under shelter.
2 Put the frozen parts into water at 40 °C (104 °F).
3 Get medical attention.

✘ **Avoid movement**: keep the frozen parts still in the water and do not massage them.

Management of frostbite

HEAT EXHAUSTION

Heat exhaustion is caused by excessive loss of fluid and salt from the body. The following features are displayed.

Features

- Pale, clammy skin.
- Faintness.
- Dizziness.
- Headaches.
- Nausea.
- Muscle cramps.
- Rapid pulse.
- Fast, shallow breathing.

Treating heat exhaustion

1 The victim should lie down in a cool place. **2** Elevate the legs (**a**). **3** The victim should, slowly but continuously, drink weak salt water (**b**) (at a ratio of half a level teaspoon of salt per litre of water) until his condition improves. **4** Call a doctor.

Treating heat exhaustion

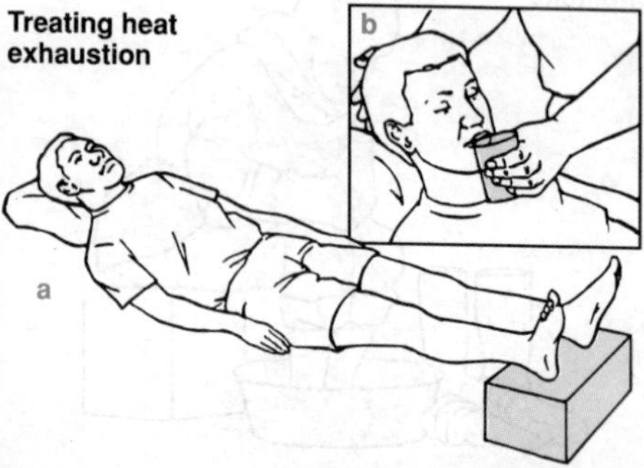

Falling unconscious

If the victim falls unconscious, put them into the recovery position (see p. 31–3) and call a doctor.

Fainting

Fainting is a brief loss of consciousness due to a temporary shortage of blood to the brain. This usually occurs because of widening of the blood vessels of the body, so that the blood volume is inadequate to maintain the pressure in the uppermost parts. Occasionally, a faint is caused by an undue slowing of the heart. More usual causes, however, are listed below.

Causes

- Stuffy or overheated atmospheres.
- Prolonged standing.
- Fear or severe distress.
- Pain.
- Prolonged coughing.
- Straining during defaecation.

A victim will usually display some of the following features.

Features

- Pallor.
- Sweating.
- Dizziness.
- Dimming of vision.
- Ringing in the ears.
- Loss of consciousness.
- Falling down.

Management of fainting

1 The victim should lie down. **2** Raise the legs high. **3** Loosen tight clothing.

✘ **Do not raise the victim** to an upright position.

Fevers

A fever is defined as a rise in body temperature above the normal 37 °C (98.6 °F). Fevers have a variety of causes.

Causes

- The most common cause is bacterial or viral infection.
- Overactive thyroid gland.
- Excessive loss of body fluid.
- Excessive heat to the head.
- Heart attack.
- Lymphoma tumour.

Treating fevers

1 Remove all clothes. **2** Sponge down repeatedly with cool-to-tepid water. **3** If feasible, put the fevered person in a cool-to-tepid bath. **4** Give aspirin, unless otherwise advised. **5** All fevers should be reported to a doctor.

✘ **Very high fever must not be allowed to persist**: it may result in brain damage.

✘ **Never give aspirin to a fevered child** under 12 years of age: it may provoke Reye's syndrome – a serious liver and brain disorder.

Foreign bodies

Children commonly put small foreign bodies – such as beads, stones, ball bearings, marbles, peas or beans – in their ears and noses. Also, objects, such as fish hooks or splinters, may acidentally become lodged in parts of the body, which need removal. Organic foreign bodies can absorb moisture and swell, so that removal becomes difficult.

FOREIGN BODIES IN THE EAR

Insects sometimes crawl or fly into the ear passage. They cannot get beyond the eardrum and remain in the outer passage, sometimes stuck to soft wax, until removed. A live insect will sometimes cause loud noises by striking the eardrum. This is harmless.

Removing insects from the ear

If it is certain that there is an insect in the ear passage, it might be floated out by gently pouring lukewarm water into the ear from a small jug. ►►

Removing insects from the ear

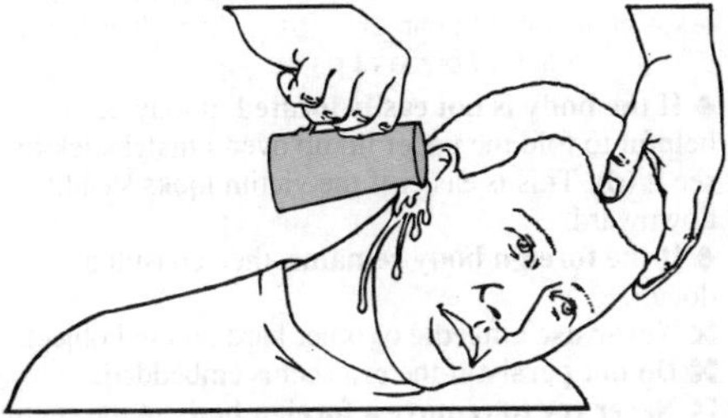

♦ **If the insect remains in the ear**, then a doctor will have to be consulted.

✖ **Do not try to remove solid foreign bodies**: attempts to do so will invariably push them further into the ear passage. Get the victim to a doctor.

FOREIGN BODIES IN THE EYE

Small foreign bodies can frequently obstruct the eye area. There are several places where they may be found.

Areas of the eye likely to be affected

- The outside of the eye.
- Behind the eyelids, where they can cause severe pain by pressing on the sensitive cornea (**a**).
- High-speed metallic foreign bodies can sometimes pass through coats of the eye and lodge in the inside.

Methods of removing foreign bodies from the eye

1 Blinking the eye under water (**b**) or in a full eyebath will often remove a foreign body.

2 A piece of grit on the inside of a lid or near the edge of the cornea can often be picked off with the corner of a folded piece of paper (**c**).

♦ **If the body is not easily located**, it may be helpful to fold the upper lid up over a matchstick to see it (**d**). This is easier if the victim looks steadily downward.

♦ **If the foreign body remains**, then consult a doctor.

✖ **Never use a needle** or other hard pointed object.

✖ **Do not persist** if the grit seems embedded.

✖ **Never try to remove a foreign body** in the centre

of the cornea. Scarring here will seriously affect vision. ►►

Foreign bodies in the eye

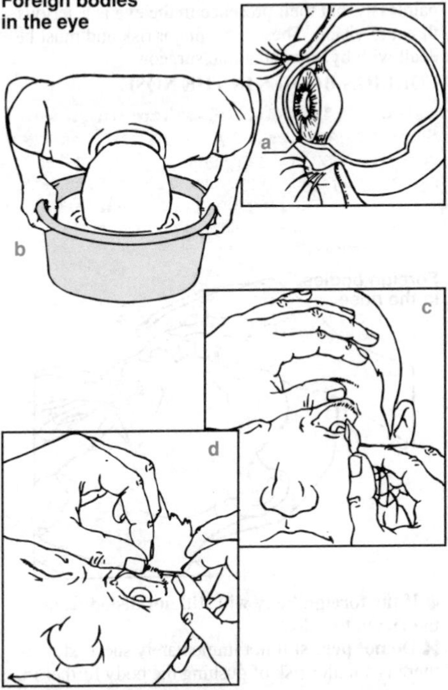

High-speed metallic foreign bodies

These tend to come from grindstones, drills, lathes or milling machines and can penetrate the eye almost painlessly, but their presence in the eye is a serious threat to vision. These are a major risk and must be dealt with by an ophthalmic surgeon.

FOREIGN BODIES IN THE NOSE

Removing foreign bodies from the nose

Small foreign bodies just inside the nostril can often be clearly seen and may sometimes be expelled by blowing the nostril on the affected side. If the victim is cooperative, and the foreign body readily visible, it may sometimes be possible to remove it with smooth tweezers.

Foreign bodies in the nose

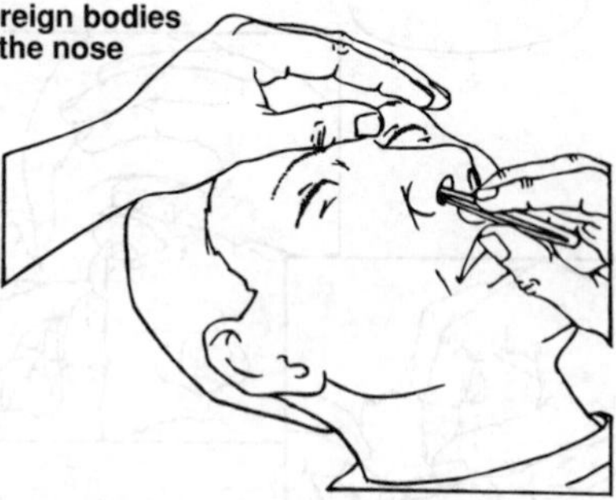

♦ **If the foreign body will still not dislodge**, take the victim to a doctor.

✘ **Do not persist** if not immediately successful, as there is a major risk of pushing the body further in.

FISH HOOKS

If the point of the buried hook lies near the surface of the skin, and medical help is not readily available, then use the following method.

✖ **Do not remove** hooks which are deeply buried.

Removing a fish hook

1 Grasp the shaft of the hook with pliers (**a**).
2 Turn the hook and push the point and barb out through the skin (**b**). **3** Cut off the barb close to the skin (**c**). **4** Pull out the hook (**d**). **5** Clean the wound thoroughly with soap and water. **6** See a doctor as soon as possible in order to avoid infection.

Removing a fish hook

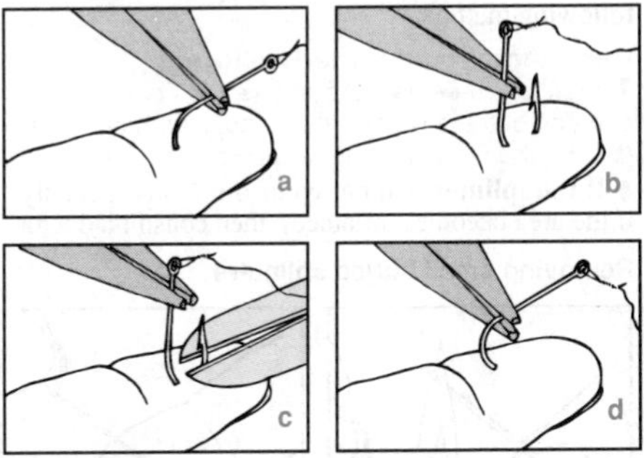

SPLINTERS

The most common foreign bodies are metal or wood splinters which have become lodged in or under the skin.

Removing protruding splinters

1 Wood and other splinters should be pulled out with tweezers if a protruding part can be grasped.
2 Wash the area thoroughly with soap and water.

Removing protruding splinters

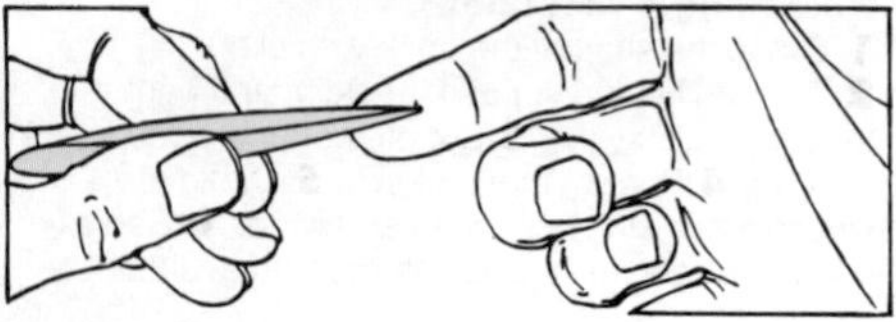

Small buried splinters

If the splinter is small and buried then use the following method.

Removing small buried splinters

1 Sterilize a needle in a flame (**a**). **2** Try to lift up one end of the splinter with the point of the needle (**b**) and then grasp it with tweezers.

♦ **If the splinter will not come out** (and especially if the area becomes inflamed), then consult a doctor.

Removing small buried splinters

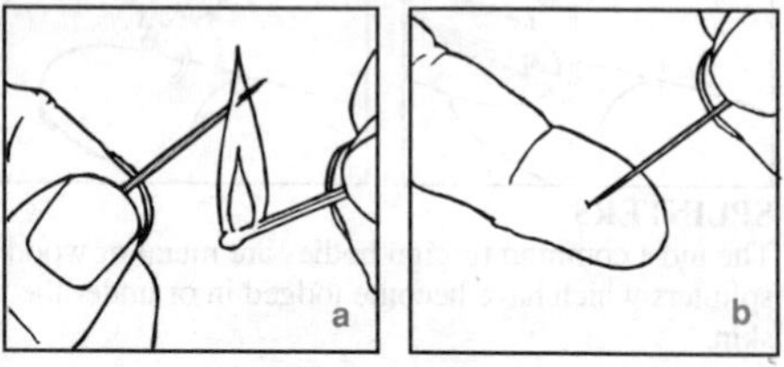

Nausea and vomiting

Nausea and vomiting suggest irritation or distention of the stomach or bowel from any of a number of causes, some of which are listed below. In most cases the vomiting will relieve the symptoms and recovery will occur spontaneously.

Causes

- Overeating.
- Excessive alcohol consumption.
- Food poisoning (see pp. 171–3).
- Gastroenteritis.
- Stomach or duodenal ulcer.
- Appendicitis.

Relieving nausea and vomiting

1 Avoid food. **2** Drink bland liquids only (water or milk), and in small quantities. **3** Note and report other symptoms.

◆ **If the nausea is unexplained** and continues for longer than a day, then call a doctor.

◆ **If the vomiting is unexplained** and continues for more than an hour, then call a doctor.

Suspected poisoning

If there is suspicion of poisoning (see pp. 161–73), a sample of the vomit should be kept for examination.

TRAVEL SICKNESS

Travel sickness is caused by continuous, passive, repetitive body movement in any transport vehicle. It displays the following features.

Features

- Yawning.
- Deep and rapid breathing.

- Salivation.
- Nausea.
- Abdominal discomfort.
- Pallor.
- Sweating.
- Vomiting.
- Headache.
- Dizziness.
- Fatigue.

Relieving travel sickness

1 Try to get into the fresh air. **2** Sit down with the head tilted backwards (**a**). **3** If on a boat, fix the eyes on an unmoving point, such as the horizon (**b**).

✖ **Avoid** alcohol consumption and eat only in moderation.

Relieving travel sickness

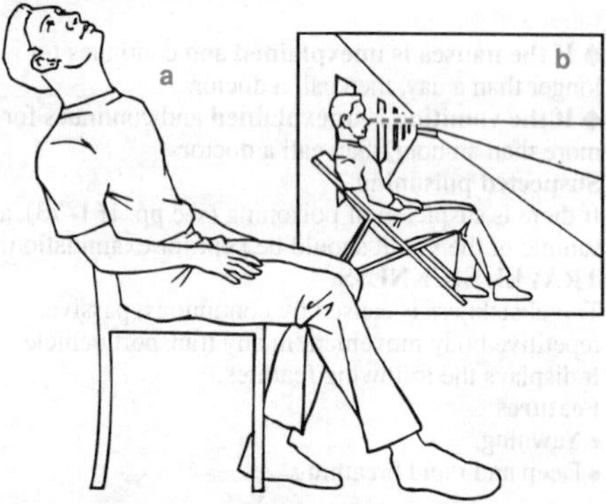

5. Dressings, bandages and slings

There are various types of dressings and bandages and a variety of ways in which to apply them, depending on the injury and the materials available. Although dressings and bandages can be bought, it is possible to improvise using towels, handkerchiefs, linen, etc.

✘ **Do not place** fluffy material directly on to a wound, as the fibres will stick to it.

Dressings

A dressing should always be large enough to cover the wound and extend for 2.5 cm (1 in) around it. If possible, it should be sterile so that no bacteria are introduced to the injury. It should also be made of a material that allows the sweat to evaporate. If sweat accumulates, the dressing becomes wet and an ideal environment for bacterial growth is created.

Functions

- To protect the wound.
- To control bleeding and to help blood to clot.
- To absorb any fluid from the wound.
- To prevent infection.

Applying dressings: rules

- The hands should be thoroughly washed.
- The wound and the surrounding skin should be thoroughly cleaned, as long as the wound is not too large and the bleeding has been controlled.

- Use extra cotton wool padding, secured with a bandage, to cover a field dressing. This will absorb excess fluid and help to control bleeding.
- Replace a dressing that may have slipped from the wound to an uncleansed area of skin with a new dressing. This will prevent infection.
- Always place a dressing *directly* on to a wound.

✖ **Do not slide** a dressing on to a wound from uncleansed skin.

✖ **Do not touch** the wound or any part of the dressing that will come into contact with it.

✖ **Do not talk** or cough over a wound or dressing.

PLASTERS (ADHESIVE DRESSINGS)

These have an adhesive backing (**a**), to which is attached a square cellulose or gauze pad (**b**), covered with protective strips (**c**). It is the pad which is placed directly on to the wound. Plasters are available in sterile wrappings and come in various shapes and sizes. They will not stick to the area around the wound unless it is clean and dry.

A plaster

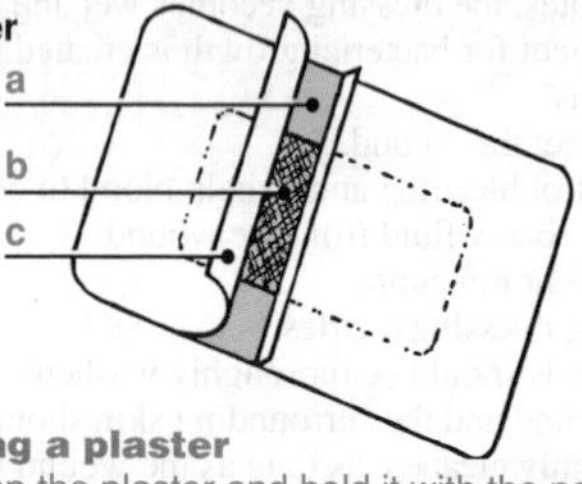

Applying a plaster

1 Unwrap the plaster and hold it with the pad downwards. **2** Peel back the two protective strips, but do not remove them (**a**) and do not touch the gauze pad. **3** Place the gauze pad on the wound. **4** Remove the protective strips completely and press the edges of the plaster down (**b**).

Applying a plaster

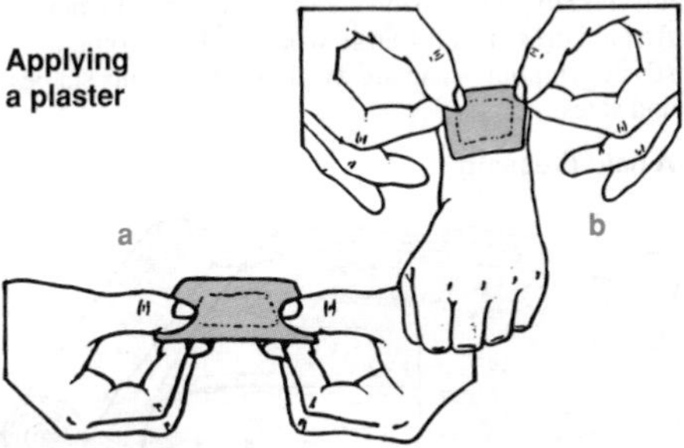

Adhesive fabric tape

Rolls of this tape come in various sizes. It should be used to secure non-adhesive dressings, if there are no bandages available, or if bandages are difficult to apply.

Adhesive fabric tape

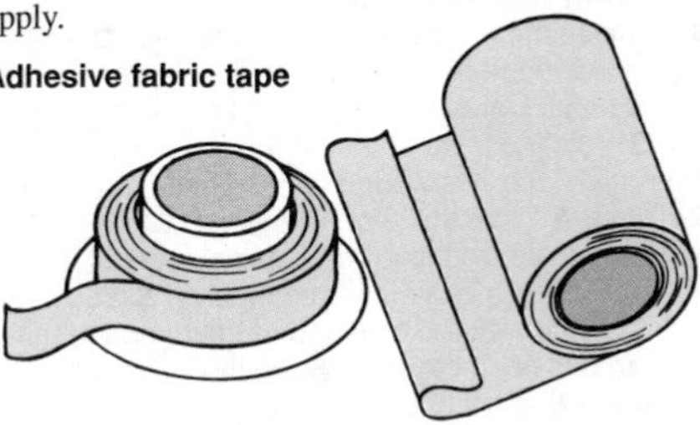

FIELD (STERILE) DRESSINGS

These are dressings which, for the sake of convenience and efficient application, have layers of gauze (**a**) and cotton-wool padding (**b**) already attached to a roller bandage (**c**). These are the best first aid dressings for large wounds. They come in sterile wrappings and are available in various shapes and sizes.

A field dressing

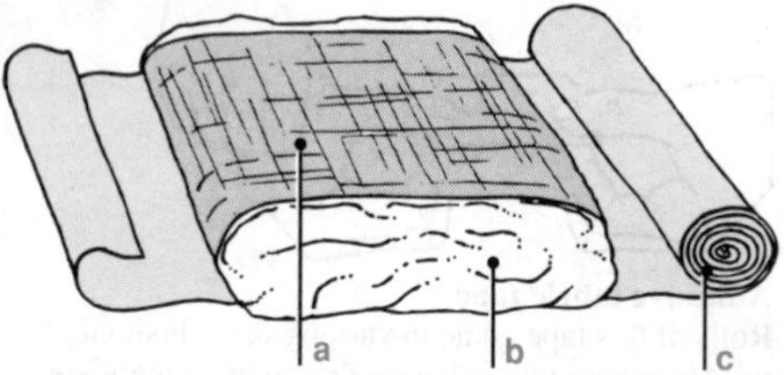

Applying a field dressing

1 Remove the inner and outer wrappings. **2** The special bandage and folded dressing should be held in one hand. Unravel the short end of the bandage (**a**). **3** Hold the ends of the bandage so that the dressing is over the wound (**b**). Open out the folded dressing. **4** Wrap the short end of the bandage around the affected limb (**c**), leaving some of it free (to be tied at the end of the procedure). **5** Securely bind the limb with the long end of the bandage until the pad has been covered. **6** Tie the two ends together (**d**) to secure the dressing.

Applying a field dressing

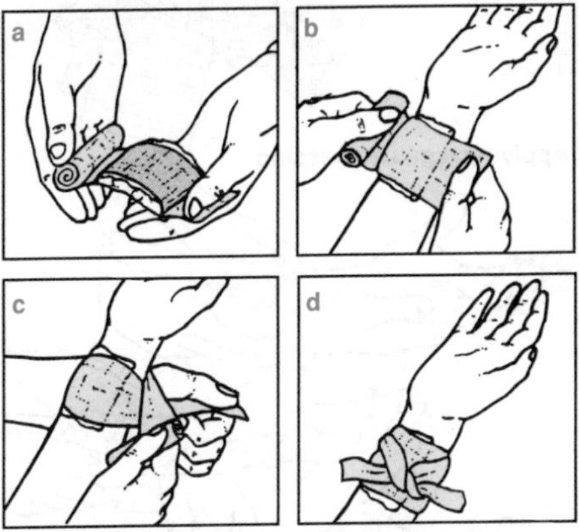

GAUZE DRESSINGS (see overleaf)

These are non-adhesive layers of gauze, available in sterile wrappings. They are used for large wounds that need a light covering (e.g. a burn), and can be secured with adhesive strapping. If a field dressing is not available, dress the wound in the following way.

Applying a gauze dressing (see overleaf)

1 Unwrap the gauze and hold it by its edges above the wound. **2** Place it on the wound (**a**). **3** Cover the dressing with a pad of cotton wool (**b**). **4** Fix the dressing and cotton wool in place with a bandage (**c**) (see pp. 231–2), sticky tape or adhesive fabric tape (see p. 225).

Gauze dressings

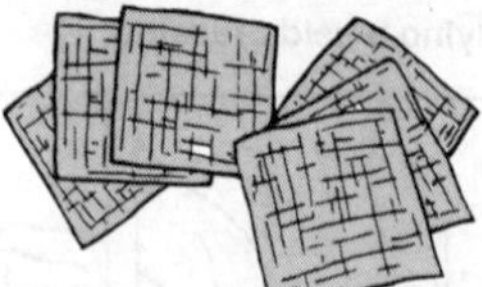

Applying a gauze dressing

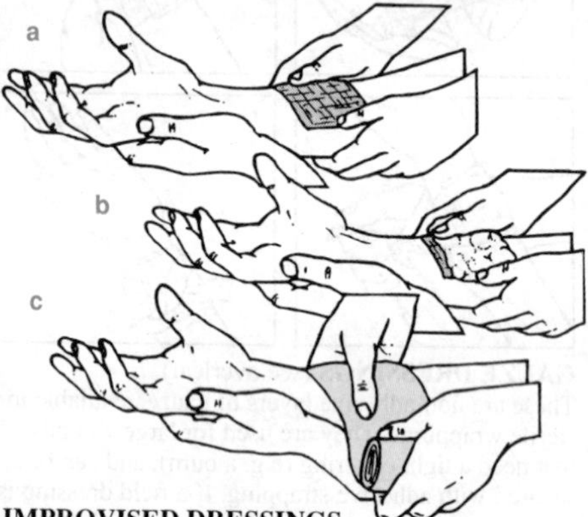

IMPROVISED DRESSINGS

If, in emergency situations, ready-made dressings are not available, any clean, dry, absorbent and non-fluffy material can be used: for example, the inside of a folded handkerchief or a newly washed towel. Folded toilet paper or tissues can also be used. These can then be secured in place with a scarf or some other similar item.

Bandages

Ready-made bandages are generally made from cotton, calico, elastic net, special paper, etc. There are two main types: roller bandages and triangular bandages.

Uses

- To maintain direct pressure and control bleeding.
- To secure dressings.
- To prevent unwanted movement of an injured limb.
- To prevent swelling.
- To support an injured limb or joint.
- To help lift and carry victims.

✘ **Bandages should not** be used for padding if softer materials are available.

Applying bandages: rules

- Apply the bandages while the victim is sitting or lying down.
- Sit or stand in front of the victim and work from his or her injured side.
- Support the injured part in the position in which it is going to be bandaged.
- When the victim is lying down, pass the bandages under the natural hollows of the ankles, knees, back and neck and ease them gently into position.
- If bandages are being used to immobilize a fracture, tie the knots on the uninjured side of the body or limb. If both sides are injured, tie the knots in the centre of the affected part.
- If a knot has to be used to secure the bandage, use a reef knot (see p. 246).
- There should be plenty of padding between the

limbs and the body, and at bony areas of the limbs (e.g. knees and ankles) before bandaging or immobilizing a fracture.

- The tissues around the injury may swell. Check the bandages frequently to make sure that they are not becoming too tight.
- When bandaging a limb, keep the finger- or toenails exposed so that they may be used to check the victim's circulation (see p. 72).
- If using a bandage to maintain direct pressure and to control bleeding, tie a knot over the pad or dressing.

✘ **Bandages should not be so tight** that they interfere with the circulation (see p. 72). They should be firm enough to control bleeding, to keep the dressing in position or to prevent movement.

ROLLER BANDAGES

A roller bandage
a head
b tail

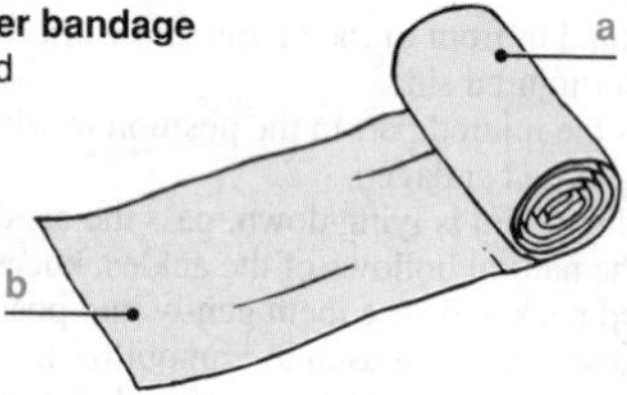

These are made of cotton, gauze or linen, and are available in rolls of up to 5 m (5 yd). They come in different widths for different parts of the body: finger – 2.5 cm (1 in); hand – 5 cm (2 in); arm – 5 or 6 cm (2 or 2½ in); leg – 7.5 or 9 cm (3 or 3½ in); trunk – 10 or 15 cm (4 or 6 in). Before the bandages are used, make sure that they are tightly rolled and of a suitable length.

APPLYING ROLLER BANDAGES

✘ **If you must** apply bandages, do so with care. Unnecessary movement of the victim may cause pain and shock. Be particularly careful to avoid movement at fracture sites.

Simple spiral bandaging

1 Support the injured part by hand in the position in which it is to be bandaged. **2** Hold the bandage with the 'head' uppermost. **3** Place the 'tail' of the bandage on the limb and begin by bandaging from below the injury upwards and from the inside of the limb outwards. Unroll only a few inches at a time. **4** Make a firm slanted turn to anchor the bandage (**a**). **5** Carry on making turns in this way. Each turn should cover two-thirds of the previous turn, with the edges parallel (**b**). **6** Use a horizontal turn to begin finishing off. **7** Fold in the edge of the bandage (**c**; see overleaf). **8** Secure it on the outside of the limb (or well away from the injury) (**d**; see overleaf). **9** Check the circulation (see pp. 21 and 72).

Simple spiral bandaging

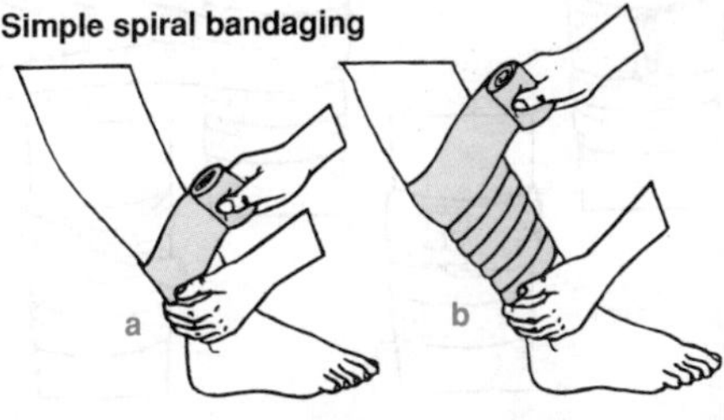

Simple spiral bandaging (continued)

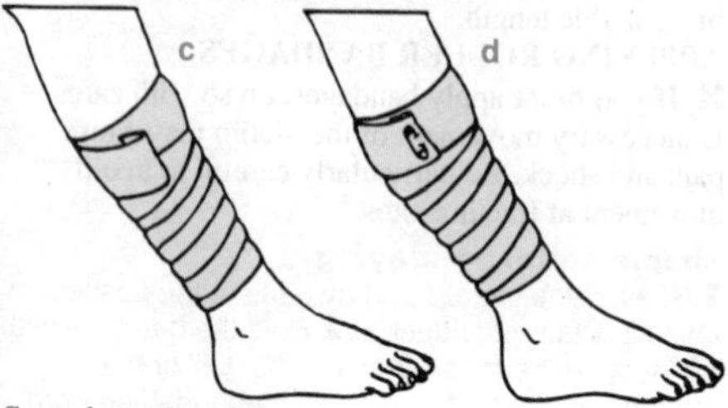

Securing a bandage

Bandages may be secured in one of three ways:
- with a safety pin (**a**);
- with sticky tape or adhesive strapping (**b**);
- by cutting the bandage, wrapping the ends (in opposite directions) around the limb, and tying them together in a reef knot (**c**) (see p. 246).

Securing a bandage

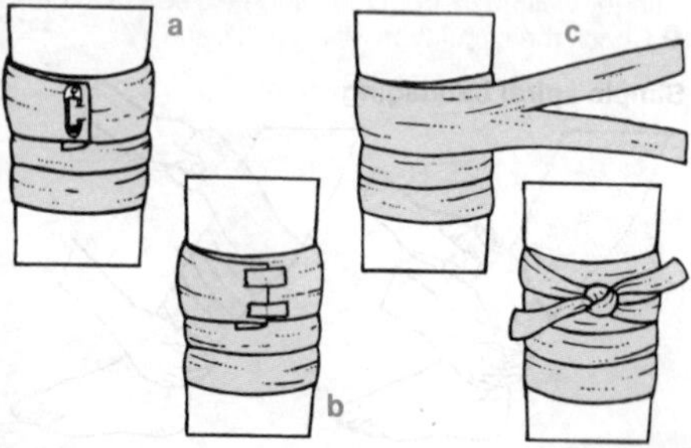

Bandaging the knee (or elbow)

1 Ask the victim to support the limb in the most comfortable position. **2** Anchor the bandage by holding the tail against one side of the kneecap. **3** Make one straight turn, taking the head over the kneecap and around the joint (**a**). **4** Carry the bandage around the upper leg, covering the top edge of the first turn (**b**). **5** Take the bandage around the lower leg covering the lower edge of the first turn. **6** Continue steps 4 and 5 but cover a little more than two-thirds of each previous turn. **7** Finish bandaging the joint by using one or two slanting turns on the upper leg, and securing the bandage on the outside of the leg (**c**). **8** Check the circulation using the toenail test (see p. 72).

Bandaging the knee (or elbow)

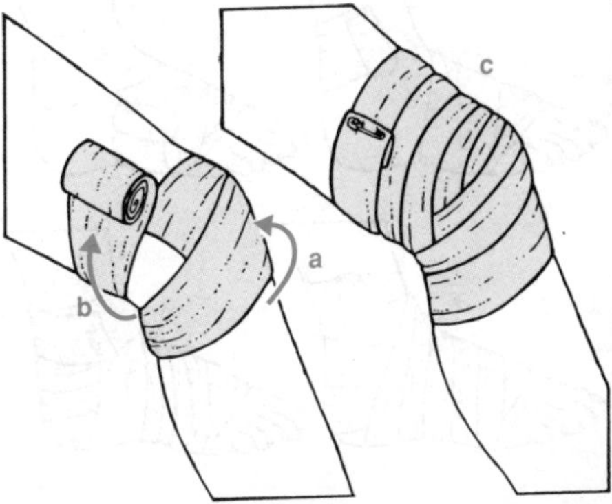

Bandaging the foot and ankle

1 Anchor the bandage by holding its tail underneath the foot, wrapping the bandage around the instep once (**a**). **2** Take the bandage from the top of the instep around the ankle, in a figure-of-eight pattern, back down over and then underneath the instep (**b**). Overlap each turn so that the instep and heel are covered and the ankle supported (**c**). **3** Finish off by using a horizontal turn around the ankle.
4 Secure the folded edge of the bandage on the outside of the ankle (**d**).

◆ **If it is only the foot that is injured**, a turn round the ankle will help to secure the bandage.

Bandaging the foot and ankle

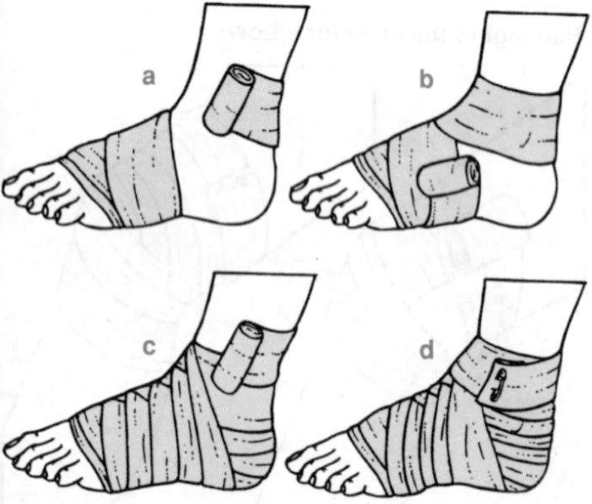

Bandaging the hand

1 Ask the victim to support the injured hand with the palm downwards. **2** Anchor the tail of the bandage to the inside of the wrist by making one horizontal turn (**a**). **3** The bandage should be taken across the back of the hand towards the base of the little finger, then around the palm of the hand under the fingers (**b**). **4** Take the head of the bandage over the backs of the fingers horizontally so that its top edge is aligned with the bottom of the little finger's nail (**c**). **5** Bring the bandage down around the palm again and diagonally across the back of the hand towards the wrist. **6** Cover the hand using these figure-of-eight turns. **7** Finish with a horizontal turn at the wrist. **8** Secure the bandage on the back of the wrist (**d**). **9** Use the fingernail test to check the circulation (see p. 72).

Bandaging the hand

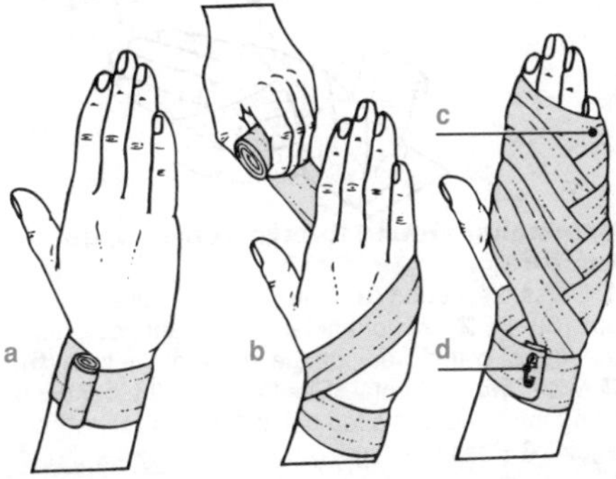

Bandaging a sprained wrist

1 Anchor the tail of the bandage to the wrist with one horizontal turn (**a**). **2** Take the bandage diagonally across the palm of the hand, in front of the thumb (**b**). **3** Carry the bandage around the back of the hand, across the palm, down to and around the back of the wrist (**c**). **4** Repeat steps 2 and 3 until the wrist is sufficiently supported. **5** Check the circulation (see p. 72).

Bandaging a sprained wrist

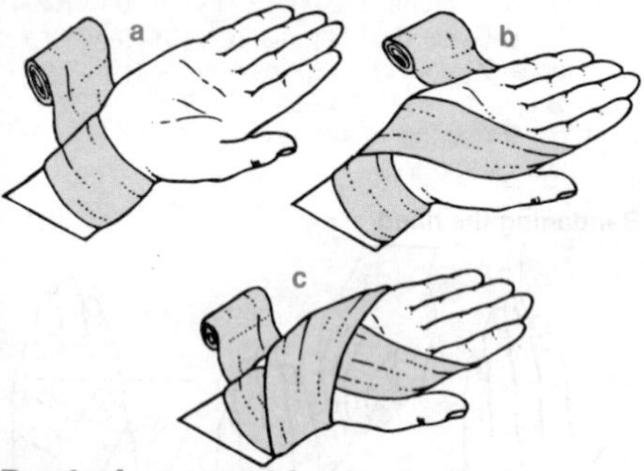

Bandaging around foreign bodies/open fractures

1 Dress the wound (**a**) (see 'Open fractures', pp. 132–3). **2** Anchor the tail of the bandage under the ring of cotton wool, on the inside of the limb (**b**). **3** Make two horizontal turns to secure the bandage. Bring the head to the top of the cotton wool pad again. **4** Pass the bandage diagonally under the limb and then up over the pad, avoiding the bone or foreign body (**c**). **5** Take it back down to the start again. **6** Continue steps 4 and 5 until the pad is secure. **7** Check the circulation (see pp. 21 and 72).

When binding an open fracture

Follow the steps above but make diagonal turns both above and below the ring pad to avoid putting too much pressure on the underside of the fracture.

Bandaging around foreign bodies/open fractures

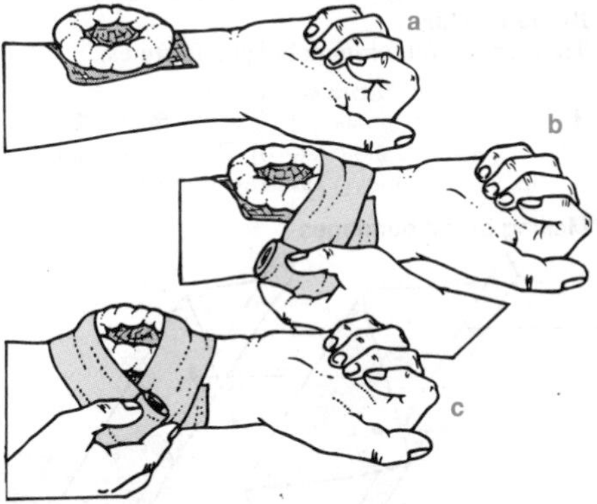

TRIANGULAR BANDAGES (see overleaf)

Although these can be bought, it is possible to make them by cutting a piece of material (such as linen or calico), of not less than 1 m^2 (1 yd^2), diagonally in half.

A triangular bandage
a point
b end
c base

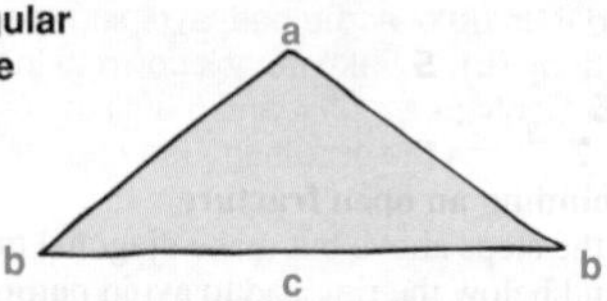

Uses

- As slings for support and/or protection.
- For securing dressings on the head, hand or foot.
- To make broad and narrow bandages.

APPLYING TRIANGULAR BANDAGES

Broad bandages

These are useful for immobilizing fractures.

Making broad bandages

1 Fold the base, making a narrow hem (**a**). **2** Fold the point towards the base (**b**). **3** Fold the whole bandage in half again in the same direction (**c**).

Making broad bandages

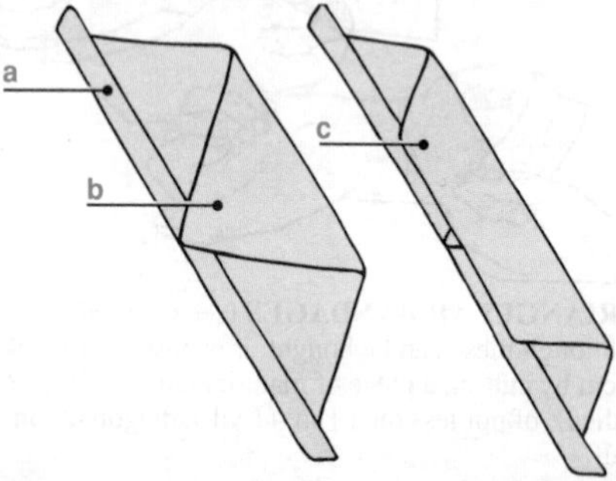

Narrow bandages

These are useful for securing dressings at wrist or ankle joints, if no other type of bandage is available, and for applying as a figure-of-eight bandage to the feet and ankles when immobilizing a fracture.

Making narrow bandages

1 Make a broad bandage. **2** Fold the broad bandage in half again (towards the base).

Applying a figure-of-eight bandage

1 Pass one end of a narrow bandage under the natural hollows of the ankles, until equal lengths of the bandage lie on either side of the ankles (**a**).

2 Cross the bandage above the ankles (**b**).

3 Wrap the ends around the feet and secure the narrow bandage under the soles of the feet with a reef knot (**c**).

Applying a figure-of-eight bandage

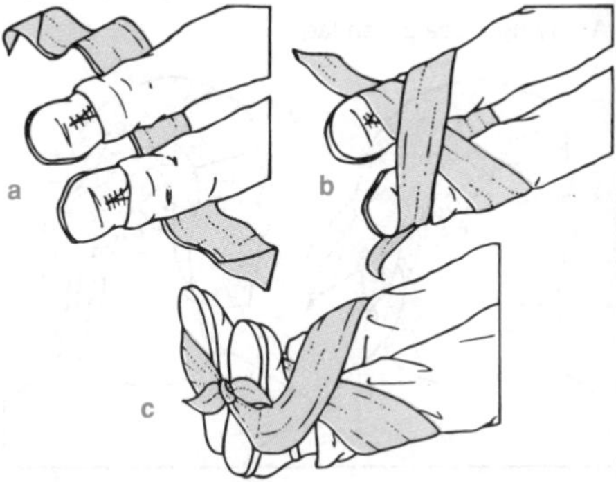

Scalp bandage

Triangular bandages are used on the scalp to hold dressings in place, not to control bleeding.

Applying a scalp bandage

1 Fold a hem along the base of the triangular bandage. **2** Place the bandage so that the centre of the base is above the space between the eyebrows (**a**). The point and the ends of the bandage should hang down at the back of the victim's head. **3** Cross the ends of the bandage at back of the head, on top of the point (**b**), and take them round to the front. The point of the triangular bandage should be left hanging down under the crossed-over ends.
4 Tie the ends on the forehead using a reef knot (**c**) (see p. 246). **5** Gently pull the point down, steadying the head with your other hand, to tighten the bandage. **6** Bring the point up and pin it to the bandage on the crown of the head (**d**).

Applying a scalp bandage

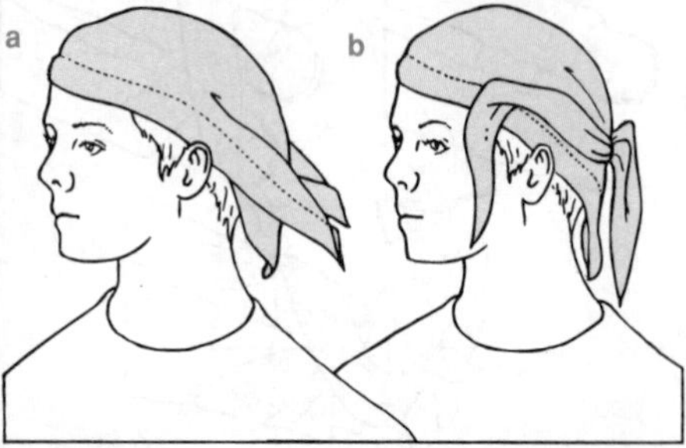

Applying a scalp bandage (continued)

c d

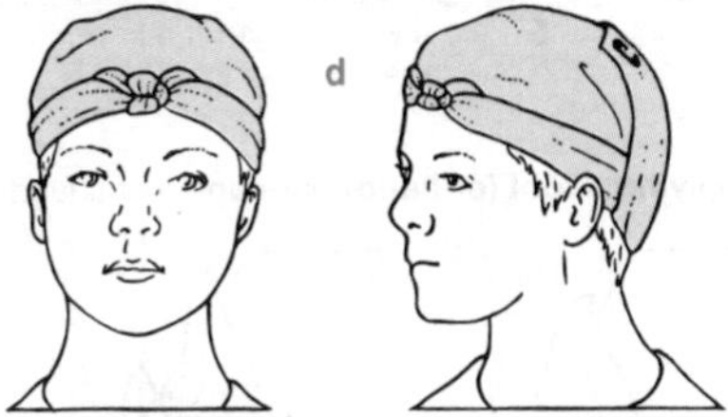

Foot (or hand) bandage

Triangular bandages are used on the hand or foot when dressings need to be held in place, and direct pressure does not need to be maintained.

Applying a foot (or hand) bandage

1 Place the victim's foot on a triangular bandage, so that the point is pointing away from the victim, in the direction of the toes and fingers, and the base (when folded upwards) covers the victim's heel and ankle (or heel of the hand) (**a**). **2** Bring the point up so that it is resting on the lower half of the shin. **3** Bring the ends of the bandage to the front of the foot, cross them over. **4** Take the ends behind

Applying a foot (or hand) bandage

a

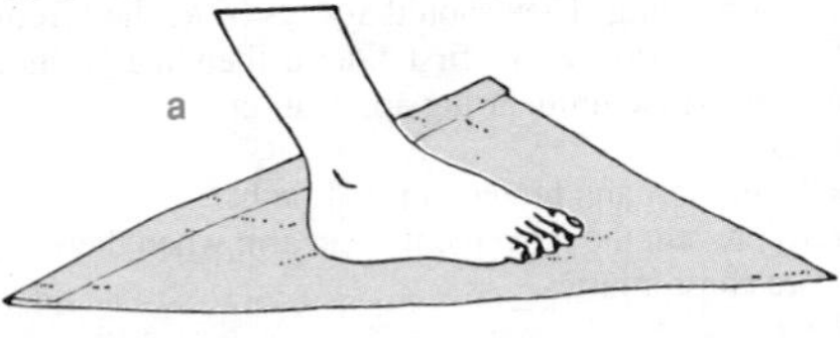

the ankle, cross them over, bringing them round to the front again (**b**). **5** Tie them in a reef knot over the point (**c**). **6** Fold the point over the knot, and secure it to the bandage over the instep with a safety pin (**d**).

Applying a foot (or hand) bandage (continued)

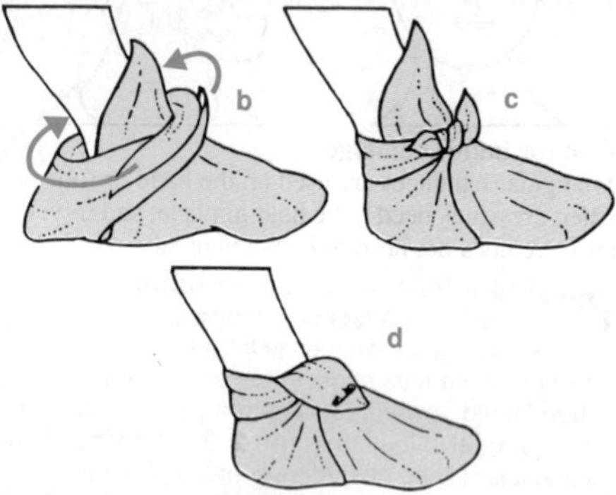

Slings

There are two types of sling: the arm sling and the elevation sling. They should always be applied from the injured side, as the first aider is then in a position to support the limb during application.

Uses

- To support and protect injured limbs.
- To prevent the movement of an arm when there are chest injuries.

ARM SLING

This type of sling is only effective if the casualty sits or stands. It keeps the forearm in place across the chest. If correctly applied, the victim's hand will be a little higher than the elbow and the fingers, from the lower knuckles onwards, should be visible.

Applying an arm sling

1 The casualty should sit down. Ask him or her to support his or her own arm once you have positioned it, with the hand a little higher than the elbow. **2** Taking one end of a triangular bandage, slide one end between the forearm and chest until the point is level with elbow but with some material

Applying an arm sling (continued overleaf)

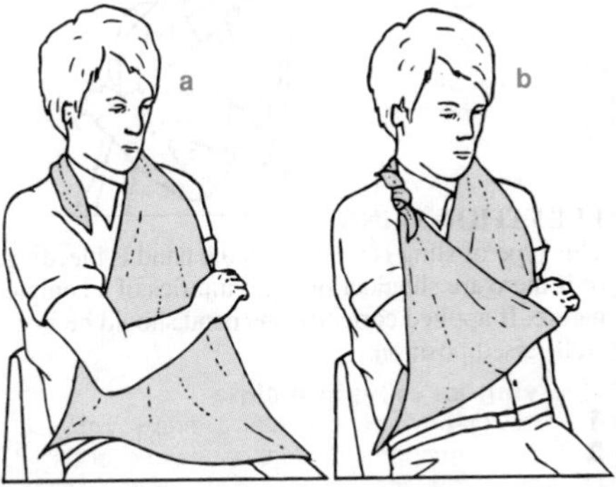

overlapping. **3** Draw the top end up over the shoulder on the uninjured side, round behind the neck, and down over the shoulder on the injured side (**a**; see p. 243). **4** Bring the lower end up over the forearm and secure it to the other end (**b**; see p. 243) with a reef knot (see p. 246) tied just above the collarbone. **5** Bring the point forward and pin it to the front of the bandage (**c**). **6** Check the circulation (see pp. 21 and 72) and adjust the bandage and/or sling if necessary.

✖ **Support the forearm** throughout this procedure.

Applying an arm sling (continued)

ELEVATION SLING

This type of sling is used when the hand is bleeding, or if there are shoulder or chest injuries of a complex nature. If applied correctly, the hand should be in a well-raised position.

Applying an elevation sling

1 Follow step 1 for applying an ordinary arm sling. **2** Position an open triangular bandage over the forearm so that one end covers the hand, several inches of which reach beyond the finger tips. The point should cover the elbow with plenty of overlap (**a**). **3** Gently put the base of the bandage under the forearm, elbow and hand (**b**). **4** Take the other end around the victim's back and over the shoulder on the uninjured side. Hold the end in place. **5** With your other hand, very gently draw up the end over the fingers of the injured limb to meet the end lying over the shoulder (**c**; see overleaf). **6** Tie the ends together in a reef knot (see p. 000) just above the collarbone. **7** Tuck the point between the arm and the front of the sling. **8** Pin the fold to the sling over the upper arm (**d**; see overleaf).

Applying an elevation sling

Applying an elevation sling (continued)

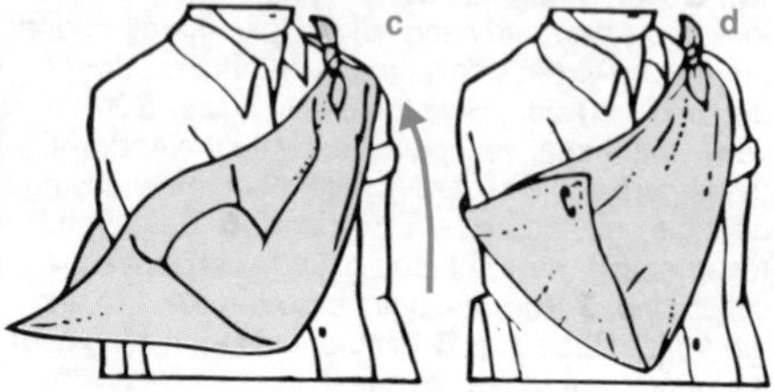

REEF KNOTS

Tying reef knots

1 Hold one end of the bandage in each hand. **2** Take the left end over and then under the right end (**a**). **3** Take what is now the right end over and under the left end (**b**). **4** Pull the knot tight (**c**).

Tying reef knots

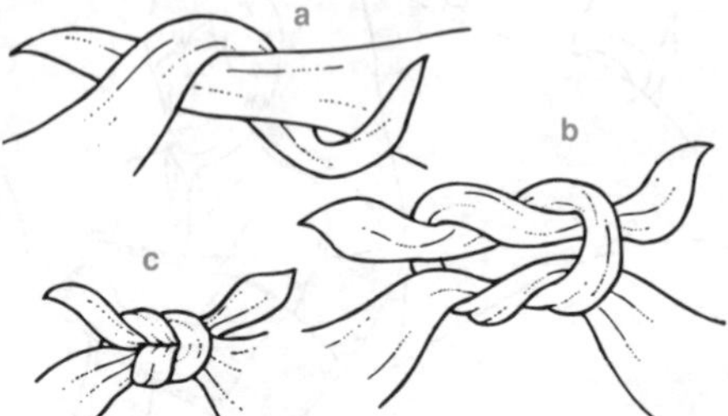

6. Useful aids

FIRST AID KIT

Kits can be bought from a chemist's shop. One can easily be made, however. The contents of a first aid kit should be kept in a suitable plastic container, such as a large sandwich box with a good, tight-fitting and secure lid. This makes the kit suitable both for travelling and for being kept in the medicine cabinet at home. A list of items that you may wish to include is given below.

- 2 large, 2 small sealed, sterile field dressings for covering wounds.
- 1 large packet of sterile, sealed plasters (adhesive dressings) of large size.
- 1 packet of smaller sterile, sealed plasters (adhesive dressings) of various sizes.
- 2 sealed packets of 10 sterile 10 cm x 10 cm (4 in x 4 in) plain gauze for dressing wounds.
- 1 roll of 2.5 cm (1 in) wide elastoplast or rayon adhesive tape.
- 1 flat tin of sterile paraffin-coated gauze for blisters and large grazes.
- 3 triangular bandages for immobilizing fractures and sprains.
- 4 large, open-weave gauze bandages.
- 2 packets of sterile cotton wool swabs for cleaning cuts, grazes, etc.
- 2 rolls of non-sterile cotton wool, for cleaning wounds and for padding.
- 1 bottle of paracetamol painkiller tablets.

- 1 clinical thermometer.
- 1 pair of flat-ended tweezers, without serrations, for removing foreign bodies.
- 1 pair of scissors, with round ends for cutting bandages and plasters.
- Safety pins of various sizes.
- 1 plastic bottle of antiseptic solution for cleaning wounds, cuts and grazes.
- 1 tube of hydrocortisone cream for insect bites, nettle rash, etc.

First aid kit: selected items

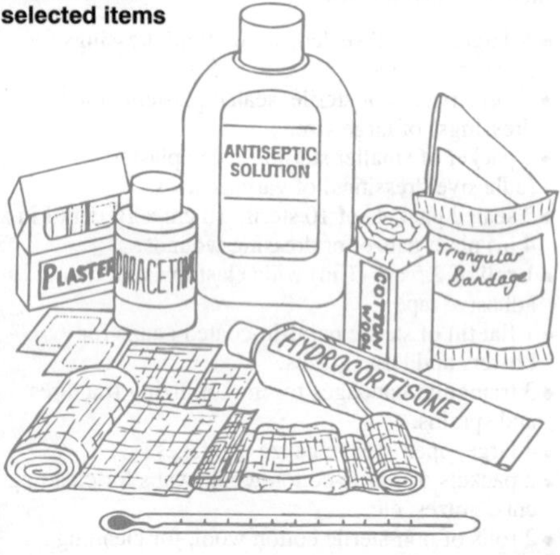

MEDICINES IN THE HOME

Prescription and non-prescription medicines should be kept in a safe place. A cupboard that is in a cool, dry position, well out of reach of children and fitted with a child-proof lock makes the ideal medicine cabinet. Only medical aids should be kept inside it. Medicines should always be stored in the medicine cabinet and never left lying around. They should be safely disposed of if they are old or no longer used.

Contents of the medicine cabinet

- Emergency telephone numbers: doctor, hospital and local chemist's shop.
- First aid kit.
- Prescription and non-prescription medicines.

Common problems and medicinal remedies

Problem	Remedy
Bites and stings	Hydrocortisone cream Hydrogen peroxide
Colds	Decongestant nose drops Antihistamine tablets
Cuts and grazes	Antiseptic cream or solution
Constipation	Laxatives: osmotics (e.g. Duphalac); lubricants (e.g. glycerine suppositories)
Diarrhoea	Anti-diarrhoeal drugs (e.g. loperamide capsules) Preparations containing kaolin

Problem	Remedy
Fever	Temperature-lowering drugs: aspirin; paracetamol (paracetamol mixture for children)
Sore throat	Throat lozenges Antiseptic mouthwash
Sunburn and rash	Anti-inflammatory lotions and creams: calamine lotion; hydrocortisone cream
Wound cleaning	Antiseptic solution

Guide to administering medicines

Non-prescription medicines. With medicines that are sold over the counter, the directions for taking them should be read very carefully.

Prescription medicines. With these, find out from your doctor or chemist whether

- they can be used with alcohol;
- they induce sleep;
- it is safe to drive or operate machinery whilst taking them;
- they can be used with the contraceptive pill;
- there are any other medicines that should not be taken at the same time.

Also, check

- when and how often they should be taken;
- whether or not they can be taken on an empty stomach, and how long after a meal a person should wait before taking them.

DRUGS GLOSSARY

Analgesics

Painkilling drugs, such as aspirin, paracetamol and neurofen.

✖ **Children under 12** should not be given aspirin except on medical advice.

Antibiotics

These are drugs that can kill bacteria. They can be taken internally or applied to the skin.

✖ **Overuse of antibiotics** can mean a risk of an allergic reaction or the development of antibiotic-resistant bacteria.

Anti-convulsants

These control epilepsy.

Anti-depressants

These drugs are mood altering, and are prescribed to depressed people.

Anti-diabetic drugs

These stimulate the production of insulin or are taken to replace it.

Anti-diarrhoeal drugs

These are used to manage diarrhoea. They slow the action of the bowel or make the stools more solid.

Anti-emetics

These are used to treat nausea and vomiting.

Antihistamines

These reduce swelling, and are used internally to treat allergies, asthma, insect bites and stings, and nettle rash (hives). They are also used to prevent travel sickness.

✖ **Antihistamines can cause** drowsiness and this may be dangerously increased if alcohol is taken.

Antispasmodics
These stop muscles from going into spasms. They relax the muscles of the intestines and lungs, and are used to treat some types of asthma.

Barbiturates
These are sedatives which depress brain activity.

✘ **Barbiturates are habit forming** and widely abused.

Benzodiazepines
See **Tranquillizers** (below).

Corticosteroids
These are used to reduce inflammation externally and internally. They are available as nose drops, sprays (for asthma), hydrocortisone creams, injections and oral preparations.

✘ **Large amounts** taken internally can mean loss of calcium from the bones, an increase in weight, abnormal skin markings and a roundness in the shape of the face.

Diuretics
These drugs encourage urination.

Heart and blood pressure drugs
Digitalis drugs are used to treat heart failure, and irregular and rapid heartbeat. Blood pressure drugs include diuretics.

Laxatives
These drugs encourage the passing of stools. They act in three ways: by increasing the bulk of the stools; by softening and lubricating the stools; by stimulating bowel action.

Tranquillizers
These are used to treat anxiety, together with anti-